MAKING MONEY FROM WRITING

G000163324

How To Books on Successful Writing

Copyright & Law for Writers
Creating a Twist in the Tale
Creative Writing
How to be a Freelance Journalist
How to Publish a Book
How to Publish a Newsletter
How to Start Word Processing
How to Write a Press Release
How to Write & Sell Computer
    Software
How to Write for Television
Improving Your Written English
Making Money from Writing
Mastering Business English
Researching for Writers
Starting to Write
Writing & Publishing Poetry

Writing & Selling a Novel
Writing a Nonfiction Book
Writing a Pantomime
Writing a Report
Writing a Textbook
Writing an Assignment
Writing an Essay
Writing Business Letters
Writing Erotic Fiction
Writing for Publication
Writing Reviews
Writing Romantic Fiction
Writing Science Fiction, Fantasy &
    Horror
Writing Short Stories & Articles
Writing Your Dissertation

Other titles in preparation

The How To Series now contains more than 200 titles in the following categories:

Business & Management
Computer Basics
General Reference
Jobs & Careers
Living & Working Abroad

Personal Finance
Self-Development
Small Business
Student Handbooks
Successful Writing

Please send for a free copy of the latest catalogue for full details (see back cover for address).

SUCCESSFUL WRITING

MAKING MONEY FROM WRITING

How to become a freelance writer

Carole Baldock

How To Books

Cartoons by Mike Flanagan

British Library Cataloguing in Publication Data
A catalogue record for this book is available from the British Library.

© Copyright 1998 by Carole Baldock.

First published in 1998 by How To Books Ltd, 3 Newtec Place,
Magdalen Road, Oxford OX4 1RE, United Kingdom.
Tel: (01865) 793806. Fax: (01865) 248780.

Note: The material contained in this book is set out in good faith for
general guidance and no liability can be accepted for loss or expense
incurred as a result of relying in particular circumstances on statements made
in this book. The law and regulations may be complex and liable to change,
and readers should check the current position with the relevant authorities
before making personal arrangements.

Produced for How To Books by Deer Park Productions.
Typeset by PDQ Typesetting, Stoke-on-Trent, Staffs.
Printed and bound by Cromwell Press, Trowbridge, Wiltshire.

Contents

List of Illustrations

Preface

The aim of this book is to discuss the following:

- Why do people want to write?
- What are they going to write?
- Where they are going to get their work published/who do they want to write for?
- How do they get their work published?
- And – when do they get paid?

READING AND WRITING TODAY

Nowadays, writing is one of the few things which virtually anybody can turn their hand to; probably more opportunities exist for writers than at any other time. This does *not* mean that you should immediately wrap up your 29,000-page masterpiece and bung it in the post to the first publisher you come across. Most things work out better for the sake of a little forward thinking.

The *Sunday Times* cites figures for the amount of time the average woman spends reading each year: five days. Men spend four-and-a-half days reading and seventeen days 'doing nothing'. Yet while sales of *The Runaway Jury* by John Grisham topped 110,000 halfway through the year, sales of the popular science title, the bestselling *Longitude* by Dava Sobel, trebled that in twelve months. Meanwhile, Maeve Binchy's *Evening Class* sold 18,000 copies in one week.

And although publishers' catalogues and shelves in bookshops seem to be full of popular fiction written by women, bestsellers by male authors outsell them: twice as many in paperback, two-thirds in hardback (see Figure 1). As one well-known authoress pointed out, however, male writers tend to garner reviews far more than female writers; one Sunday supplement recently reviewed seventeen books by men and one edited by a woman. Yet there always will be a demand. Many people still prefer to pick up a book and settle down in a comfy chair rather than peer at a computer screen. Despite

Pos	Prev Pos	Title	Author
1	1	Appassionata	Cooper, Jilly
2	4	The Runaway Jury	Grisham, John
3	3	The English Patient	Ondaatje, Michael
4	2	The English Patient (film tie-in)	Ondaatje, Michael
5	8	Little Book of Calm	Wilson, Paul
6	0	Tales from Herodotus	Herodotus
7	6	High Fidelity	Hornby, Nick
8	5	Last Orders	Swift, Graham
9	19	Fever Pitch	Hornby, Nick
10	10	Notes from a Small Island	Bryson, Bill
11	12	Gardens of England and Wales	
12	188	Natwest Playfair Cricket Annual	
13	15	Crown of Swords	Jordan, Robert
14	13	Men Are from Mars, Women are from Venus	Gray, John
15	100	How I Got My Shrunken Head	Stine, R L
16	11	Sophie's World	Gaarder, Jostein
17	27	Highway Code	Transport, Dept of
18	40	Girl Power: The Official Book of the Spice Girls	Spice Girls
19	28	Take Care of Yourself	Sach, Penelope
20	23	Writing Home	Bennett, Alan

Fig. 1. In the bestseller lists male authors tend to outsell female writers. (Taken from *The Bookseller*.)

controversy over standards of education and the worrying fall of literacy, nearly everybody at some points reads something:

- comics
- newspapers
- magazines
- journals
- poetry
- non-fiction books
- novels.

Magazines alone can be divided into weekly, fortnightly, monthly, bi-monthly, quarterly, twice-yearly and annual. As for the approximate 150,000 books published annually, a breakdown of recent figures make interesting reading:

1. Fiction: just over 9,000.
2. Children's books: 8,000.
3. School textbooks: 3,500; education: 2,000.
4. Biography and literature: 3,000 each.

All the rest, from art to travel, are non-fiction, the biggest selling areas (over 4,000 each) being economics, history, religion and social sciences, followed by computers and medicine. Since leisure and information are two of the main growth industries of the 20th century, reading continues to play an important role. And if people want to read, somebody has to write the books.

Carole Baldock

1
Writing Opportunities
for Freelances

UNDERSTANDING WHY YOU WANT TO WRITE

In *Writing for Magazines*, Jill Dick mentions a recent survey about home-based occupations, the most popular being – writing. And according to Celia Brayfield, in *Bestseller*, another survey confirms that one in ten people really do think they have a book inside them. What's more amazing is that one in fifty *have* written one.

Often a love of reading encourages people to start writing, but there are many reasons for taking it up, whether as a hobby, something which you always quite fancied doing, or a career, even as a kind of vocation. For some people, writing is as vital as breathing. Nor do you need to be a genius to have success as a writer. It must be understood that writing is a craft, one that needs mastering, but is well within the grasp of most people. As are ideas. Inspiration is no will o' the wisp, even if that is how it is pictured (at least by poets) it is all around us. You can train your eye, and your mind, to pin it down.

Taking up writing
People take up writing for many reasons:

- To express themselves creatively.
- For therapeutic reasons; because it's relaxing.
- It's something they enjoy as a hobby.
- To provide information, or for entertainment.
- To see their name in print.
- To make their mark on the world, leaving something for posterity.
- As a means of becoming rich and famous.
- Because, in the immortal words of Stephen King: 'Not to write is a kind of suicide'.

You may not agree with this last (particularly if you don't care for horror stories) but although it appears frighteningly intense, that's how some writers feel. It doesn't necessarily guarantee success, any more than it does for the person who wakes up one morning thinking 'I'll have a go at bashing out a story after lunch.' All or any of the above are valid reasons for writing, but some are more realistic than others.

Assessing your strengths and weaknesses

Nobody embarks on a hobby unless they enjoy doing it, yet writing often appears to be the exception which proves the rule, because of the dreaded writer's block. There are few things worse than yearning to write and finding inspiration has locked itself away and refuses to come out. Lack of motivation is as painful, and it's nerve-wracking when deadlines are looming. Fortunately, panicking tends to kick-start the brain into gear, although it doesn't necessarily make things easier. It's wonderful to feel that you can't wait to get cracking, but the very thought of finishing off a certain poem or approaching a tricky chapter can make you unutterably miserable. Consolation comes only with the blissful sense of relief once you have got the work done. It *will* get done, if only by default such as something much worse cropping up, which makes the original look like a doddle.

Reasons for writing

So you love reading, you were always good at English at school, and there are a few ideas floating around your head which you think are worth looking out pen and paper for to jot down. Maybe you've just finished somebody's latest bestseller and slammed it shut, echoing David Bowie's words '*I* could do better than that!' Whether uttered with determination, resentment or bewilderment – 'Why on *earth* do they print such rubbish?' – or scorn, some authors are famously known to have been thus inspired.

Improving basic skills

Having decided that you really do fancy writing, take a good look at your qualifications. Don't lose heart, because there are plenty of ways to improve your skills:

- writing magazines
- books
- workshops
- classes
- correspondence courses.

You can learn, or teach yourself, from scratch by:

- Brushing up on basic grammar, spelling and punctuation.
- Learning how to write poetry, prose and non-fiction.
- Finding out how to present your work and approach editors.
- Getting information about publishing your work.
- Learning what to do about marketing your work.

Not that publication is always the aim of all writers. Some people are perfectly content just to write, although there are those whose aims outstrip their ambitions, or who suffer from the Hamlet/ Gravedigger syndrome, *ie* possessing a gift for comedy they yearn to try a tragedy, and occasionally vice versa.

Committing yourself to the right area

Blockbusting novels are one thing, but what if you then discover a gift for writing something else? Novelists can have problems if the public clamours for the latest in a particular genre when they are dying to try their hand at something completely different. One cautionary tale tells of somebody so successful at writing for a popular soap that any attempt to take a sabbatical to tackle The Novel was thwarted by their agent. It's the stuff of storytelling, but you should establish whether you are writing for yourself, or for other people. If you have something you wish to communicate, it's important to accept that the customer (*ie* reader) is always right. You are committed to providing whatever it is they want to read, and that's the heart and soul of book publishing today.

DECIDING WHAT YOU WANT TO WRITE

People tend to take up writing for four main reasons:

- a hobby
- to earn the occasional bit of cash
- a career
- going for the big one, the blockbuster which will make you rich and famous.

The miraculous thing is that the last possibility, although remote, has been known to result from the other three. It is possible to organise your writing, mapping out your progress step by step, but it can evolve in all kinds of ways because it is a creative process.

Authors often claim their characters 'just took over', that the plot suddenly developed a life of its own. Success may seem to take a lot of luck, but you largely make your own luck as a writer. Perhaps 'serendipity' is more accurate, once you learn to recognise opportunities when they present themselves and to make the most of them. You also need the ability to work hard, be very patient and persevere.

It certainly isn't a sensible decision to opt for a full-time career as a freelance on the strength of some reviews in the local press, a couple of anecdotal articles in a parenting magazine, and because you got 80 per cent in an essay about libraries which your tutor suggested publishing in a journal *and* paid you £25. But you wouldn't be reading this book otherwise.

MAKING IT A HOBBY OR A CAREER

There are all kinds of possibilities to consider. With the world of publishing in a turmoil, the main publishing houses growing bigger all the time (too big for their books is a common view), current advice is frequently to specialise. You may feel this is restrictive: how many writers concentrate on one thing, be it poetry, fiction or non-fiction? But there is nothing to stop you specialising in several areas. Your main interest could also produce any of the following:

- fillers
- news items
- reviews
- interviews
- features
- columns/series.

Similarly, consider one or more of all these areas:

- historical
- geographical
- educational
- social
- literary
- humorous
- topical
- technological.

> **Whether you start by tackling everything which comes up, or by choosing one main area and then diversifying, in time you become more aware of your strengths.**

You learn to capitalise on your strengths and to make the most of your options.

CHECKING NATIONAL AND LOCAL DEMAND

Market research is vital. It's the only way to work out what outlets are available and whether your material matches up; always read several copies of any publication which appeals to you. It's usually best to begin slowly and work your way up, starting with small or local magazines, rather than banging on the door of *Vogue* or the *Sunday Times*. Nevertheless, it will sometimes open wide enough for you to slip your foot inside. Making the most of any opportunity, seeing the perfect match between material and magazine, could have you diving into the newsagent and triumphantly waving this month's issue in the air, the one containing your work.

Looking into newsstand opportunities

National publications have huge numbers of readers to keep happy and, consequently, an enormous appetite for material. Material, that is, of a certain kind; the odds are usually stacked against you when it comes to short stories and poetry. Editors are inundated with them whilst opportunities are extremely limited. If it is your forte, try the small/independent press (see Further Reading). Payment is invariably minute, usually non-existent, but many of these magazines have excellent reputations so publication of your work is regarded as prestigious.

With the newsstand publications, your best bet is to be an expert in your field or to come up with a good, topical idea (see Figure 2). You can't really fail with the human interest angle. Watch the daily newspapers for anything hitting the headlines (usually a court case) and note how often that story reappears, perhaps in the form of an interview with other people in similar situations or a feature with a panel of experts giving their opinion. It may surface in the women's section, the Sunday supplement, weekly or monthly magazines. Agencies rely on a network of people to scour the local press for such stories, to be offered as 'an exclusive' to the nationals – at a price.

<u>Doing it Out</u>
The recession is hitting people in every walk of life; no job is safe ...
A miner gets the sack
A chimney sweep is fired
A stripper is suspended
A footballer is kicked out
A feminist is dismissed
A soldier gets his marching orders
A short-sighted painter and decorator gets shown the door
A magician's assistant is given her cards
A parachutist is given the push
A pessimist hands in his resignation

Shorter version: medical outlet?
A pessimist hands in his
  resignation
A short-sighted painter and
  decorator gets shown the door
A soldier gets his marching
  orders
A parachutist is given the push
A stripper is suspended
A feminist is dismissed

Or that new women's mag?
A stripper is suspended
A magician's assistant is given
  her cards
A footballer is kicked out
A soldier gets his marching
  orders
A feminist is dismissed
A pessimist hands in her
  resignation

Fig. 2. Work in progress using topical ideas,
in this case originally for *The Lark*.

Just as propitious is the interview; every popular author or actor pops up everywhere publicising the latest book or film. And this is not always a cosy *tête-à-tête*, as it sometimes comes from the organisation's press packs which promote their projects.

Writing fillers
Probably the simplest way to see your name in print is to aim for the 'filler' market; that is, short pieces up to a maximum of 300 words such as:

- letters
- anecdotes/jokes
- trivia
- news items.

The chances of getting published are far greater, because fillers are popular with readers and editors usually have small spaces left in each issue. Best of all, payment works out at an amazing rate, especially if you're a quick worker, which is why this is an excellent way to begin. However, don't overlook the fact that there is an art in writing short pieces, whatever the topic and whether the style is humorous or serious.

Looking at local interest

Also recommended as a good starting point are local radio stations, in particular community radio, since they often have an even greater demand for material. As for publications, again fillers are popular, as well as articles, features and interviews. Keep them short and sweet, and focus on something of interest to the community, such as local history or reminiscence. There are greater opportunities here for your own column or series, though little chance of payment. Nonetheless, publication is a distinct possibility because magazines and newspapers abound, even in rural areas. Consider:

- local papers
- 'freebies'
- listings magazines
- student magazines
- newsletters
- trade publications.

There is usually little to choose between local papers and 'freebies' (freesheets), as they both rely on advertising. However, there may be more news in the paper, the freesheet being full of advertorials, features about local shops linked to the advertisements they have placed.

Aiming at the 18–35s

The standard age range for many magazines should not deter you from writing about a subject which interests you, even if there are lots more candles on your birthday cake. One listings magazine should be sufficient in any region, but some cater specifically for the youth market: fashion, clubs and film. They also tend to come and go; some areas may have half a dozen or so at a time, dwindling to one until another springs up. One well known listings magazine is *The Big Issue*; all three editions now pay for features and interviews, but writers tend to overlook it, assuming it's purely issue based. The contents actually need to have a wide appeal so that more people buy copies, to help the homeless.

Student magazines sometimes accept outside contributions when struggling to fill their pages, for example if exams are looming. Even schools and colleges use their desk-top publishing facilities to produce some kind of publication, mostly for the benefit of the pupils. They may welcome useful ideas, the disadvantage being that they don't publish anything during the lengthy school holidays.

Aiming for other publications

Newsletters are a staple of many organisations. Clubs and societies rely on local contributions: art, drama, film, music, hobbies or collecting. There is rarely any payment, even for the hard-pressed editor, but it's always useful experience when starting out. Getting your name in well-established newsletters makes a handy addition to your CV.

Then there's the trade press, with publications for everything from accountants to zoologists. What's more, they pay, and at reasonably good rates. Specialities come in useful because there is a huge demand for good, interesting copy, but best leave the technical stuff to the real experts.

Listing the ground rules

Having decided what you want to write, sit yourself down and get cracking – anything you can do, just go right ahead and do it. Consider some titles you may not previously have thought of (see Figure 3).

QUESTIONS AND ANSWERS

I'd rather spend my time getting on with my writing. Is reading really that important?

Reading is vital, not just for enjoyment but for education and inspiration as well. It's also one of the best ways to carry out market research, as well as giving you the chance to consider your own material from every angle and realise its full potential.

It's such a lot of hard work submitting stuff to all kinds of different outlets, hoping to get published. Is it worth all the effort?

Making a name for yourself and building on your contacts will lead to a receptive audience for any future projects, so try to make the most of every opportunity that comes along.

Fig. 3. Considering magazine outlets.

I seem to have gone though a really bad patch lately – everything's been turned down. How on earth do people learn to cope with rejection? I just feel like giving up for good.

Cheer yourself up by remembering that we all learn from our mistakes; it's the best way to improve our work. It's hard not to brood over rejection but see it as a chance for another door to open, leading to something else which may very well turn out even better.

CASE STUDIES

Dexter, Brent and Katrina are three very different people who are all interested in writing and wouldn't mind earning a bit of money, if not a living, from it.

Dexter makes the most of a funny business

Dexter has opted for early retirement, escaping from middle management and the rigours of nine-to-five. Now's his chance to start doing what he's always wanted to do, having scribbled away at different things for years. The latest was an attempt at comedy writing after interviewing international star Dolly Daydream. Hard-working, but not very sure of himself or where he is going, he has acquired a girlfriend-cum-agent, Shelley-Danielle, affectionately (and accurately) known as the She-Devil. She is trying to convince him that poetry, not comedy, is the new rock'n'roll.

Brent makes sure of lots of fun and games

Brent always did have artistic tendencies – and the temperament to go with it. Lead singer of the band Qute, (until the other members made a complete hash of the chance of being signed up by a major recording label) he's working for an entertainments magazine as deputy editor, unpaid. Not exactly making a living from writing, he's had to join a temping agency, relying on charisma and charm to get by rather than being reliable and conscientious. As they say, write about what you know, and Brent knows he can turn his experiences with the music business into a bestselling novel.

Katrina wants to make a name – and some money – for herself.

Katrina is so keen to write for a living she has never really considered any other work. She used to work for the same magazine as Brent and found it enjoyable, but she wants to move on, especially now she is part of a network, with lots of useful and interesting contacts. A regular contributor to several publications, she needs to ensure that she has a regular income. Being a freelance is fascinating, since you never know what will turn up next, although it also means constantly juggling time and money. Magazines tend to fold with depressing regularity but at least Katrina is still in business.

DISCUSSION POINTS

1. Are you able to be completely objective about your abilities? Will they match up to your aims?

2. What kind of characteristics do you think are valuable to become a writer?

3. Which writing skills are you happy with? Which of them may need some work?

ASSIGNMENT

Make a note of what writing you have done to date, then list what sort of writing you would like to do and your favourite topics.

2
Equipping Yourself

STICKING TO BASICS

All you need to become a writer is pen and paper? There's a bit more to it than that:

- making room to write
- organising your work
- polishing your skills
- building up a library
- getting to grips with computers.

A room with a view – to becoming a writer

Jane Austen wrote on a corner of a table, Roald Dahl in a garden shed. What's best for you is whatever makes you comfortable. Going 'out' to work is supposed to encourage you to be more professional, but finding anywhere accessible *and* affordable could be tricky, though at least you won't have a friend dropping in, or family or neighbours. Although people are impressed that you are a writer, they rarely appreciate your need to be alone to work. Working at home incurs problems, particularly with a pram in the hall. Husband or wife, and children, may need training to leave you in peace – just as you let them get on with hours of watching TV or shut up in their room listening to doleful CDs. Why feel guilty, when your solitude has a serious purpose?

Fond though we are of our pets, they too are a distraction. No matter how much you love cats, they're far too keen on skateboarding on your papers, prancing along the keyboard or pouncing on the mouse.

Finding the right place

Wherever you decide to create your nest, make it cosy. We all work to the best of our ability in pleasant surroundings, though a window overlooking the garden can be as much distraction as inspiration. You should only need a table and chair, with room for storing books and stationery and all the paperwork.

Popular places to work in are the bedroom (more peaceful, less practical) and the dining room. It is feasible to work in the kitchen, ignoring that mountain of dishes, or the front room, if you can be sure of a spare hour or so on a regular basis.

> **Practice helps make perfect and organisational skills make life a lot easier.**

Keeping yourself fighting fit
Healthy mind, healthy body? It does help stop you buckling under the stress of impending deadlines:

- Keep a stock of aromatherapy oils for the bath, for relaxation or revitalisation.

- Make sure the room is airy in summer, warm in winter and not stuffy.

- Take regular exercise, whether a brisk walk or a work-out; both will clear your head and aid creativity.

- Make sure your chair is at the right height; don't risk hurting your back.

- Take care of your eyesight. Don't work in poor light or for too long at the computer; two hours maximum no matter how urgent your work.

- After each session, unwind with a really good stretch.

ORGANISING YOUR WORK

Sexist or not, it is fair to say that it's harder for women to learn to re-prioritise and put writing ahead of housework. Men, mostly, have to fit writing in with a nine-to-five job. With housework, once women make their minds up that it'll have to wait, they then have to organise themselves so that some housework gets done, sometimes.

Quentin Crisp's comments about dust looking no different after four years have an irresistible ring.

Many people are put off from the start, convinced they can't find the time no matter how much desire to write is burning away inside. If it goes *that* deep, however, you will undoubtedly find a way. It's extremely offputting to hear that famous writers produce screeds of the stuff, all day, every day. It's not compulsory. Playwright Tim Firth (*Preston Front*) would be perfectly happy to produce 400 words a day – providing it's the right 400 words. That adds up to 3,000 a week, 12,000 a month, more than enough in a year to produce a book.

Writing as a habit

It's a big help to get used to writing on a regular basis – writing anything at first, if necessary. Before long, you may need to prioritise according to deadlines, with paid writing probably coming top of the list. Long-term projects like books often need daily attention, so an average day may include:

1. Working on the current chapter.
2. Tackling half a dozen letters.
3. Having a go at fillers, news items or reviews.
4. Writing a feature, the latest article in a series, a column, an interview or completing an appraisal.

That's just using the computer. Then there's the paperwork:

- dealing with the post (sorting it, sending it)
- filing
- reading/researching.

Dealing with paperwork

Making telephone calls also involves paper, when making notes. As for letters, writing them is an essential skill.

Once your correspondence starts to grow, you face a Sisyphean task because as fast as papers are dealt with (replying to letters, posting off articles and so on), more take their place. Each piece of writing seems to result in more than one more piece of work. For example, if you write an article for one publication they could request another, whilst the subject of the article might ask you for something. If another editor reads it and contacts you with some suggestions for more work, it begins to look like an avalanche of paper.

Networking – a good career move

Networking is vital for all writers:

- to survive
- to progress
- to succeed.

Writers rely on the connections they make. No matter what new piece of work you approach, you can rarely tell exactly where it will end up. It's one of the most fascinating aspects of freelancing; we all have to start somewhere, and starting points differ for everyone. However, once you pass the point of snatching the odd hour to write, some kind of programme should be drawn up. You probably won't know exactly what suits you best until you put it into practice. Take filing: it's not that important what method you use, providing you know the whereabouts of any one piece. You don't need the mind of a librarian – according to the Dewey Decimal System, Religion comes next to Computers (probably because the machine figures in your most fervent prayers) and, at one point, Feminism came under Folklore.

Mapping out a programme

One recommended method is getting it down on paper with the help of:

- diary
- calendar
- wallchart.

That way nothing gets left out, although it tends to be time-consuming. But don't dispense with every form of aide-memoire, although exercising your memory does it nothing but good. You also need to keep records of work sent out and work accepted. Try to keep everything as simple as possible, and the best method for you should evolve.

Certain times of year are much busier, usually the ends of March, June and September when there are more deadlines, from daily to quarterly publications. By contrast, there is little activity during December and August; some magazines don't appear during these months and if you're not doing much work, you won't be paid much – particularly when the accounts department is on holiday. Make the most of the lulls, taking care to have some time off as well

Monday

9.30am-10.00:	Sort post and relevant files
10.00-10.20:	Carry on with next page of short story
11.30-12.45:	Answer urgent letters; remember to take last look at article for USA journal before posting it off
12.45pm-1.10	Prepare letters for posting – are there enough IRCs?
1.10-1.30:	Lunch
1.30-2.30:	Get back to working on appraisal before you lose the plot: include summary of Chapter 7 and check on spellings
2.30:	Any really urgent phone calls
3.00-5.00:	Take letters to post then go shopping
5.00-6.00:	Make tea and wash dishes
6.00-7.00:	Tackle paperwork – find out who's borrowed that biography of Elvis?
	Select children's books from publishers' catalogues for November issue of *Event* (suggest October for next year – more in time for Christmas?)
	Make notes for article about pitfalls of working as a freelance. Try to find that file about the magazine XYZ say they're also having problems with.
	Sort out poems for reading on National Poetry Day; any suitable for next month's competitions?
7.00-7.30:	Finish off research for article about horror writers up north; compare with USA or Canadian writers?
7.30-9.00:	Reading: several pages (two chapters if possible): *Cyrano de Bergerac* before going to see play (NB where's the French dictionary got to?)
	New Welsh Review, for **Orbis** poetry index
	The Genius of Shakespeare, for **Theatre** magazine
	Emotional Blackmail, background info for schools information pack on bullying (worth testing out case studies if it stops people borrowing all my books?)
	Writers' News – remember to check details of any competitions, to update records – ask *Orbis* editor if he saw their article on vanity press?

Fig. 4. Sample daily work chart.

as tackling immense piles of papers or making up your mind which of your files can finally be dispensed with. Nowhere does hope spring quite so eternal as in a writer's heart, because we've all read stories about careers which suddenly took a surprising turn.

The simplest way to prioritise your work is to follow the lead times of the publications you contribute to:

- daily
- weekly
- fortnightly
- monthly
- bi-monthly
- quarterly.

POLISHING YOUR SKILLS

Even those who loved English at school were probably surprised to learn that writers do not simply sit down and write. For example, when studying Wilfred Owen's poems, at first it seems amazing that he went to the bother of deliberately employing devices such as alliteration and para-rhyme. People who were never keen on literature can't see what all the fuss is about correct grammar, punctuation and spelling. But what would be the response should any of the national newspapers experiment with a copy with none of the mistakes corrected, a front page headline proclaiming: 'Edukashun a nashnul dizgrace'?

Creating a good impression

Correct English has always been important, and still is today although standards of literacy are falling. Writing in private is one thing, but when writing goes public – *ie* is intended to be read – it must be correct. Some say this is inhibiting and stops people writing, but most writers want to produce work of which they can be proud, so mistakes should be corrected. Good writing creates a good impression; nobody would think very highly of a newspaper full of errors, and it would lead us to question its credibility. If spelling and grammar are wrong, how do we know that they've got their facts right?

Getting to grips with the basics

We are often nervous about things we do not know. Learning the basics of English may seem intimidating, but once learnt, it stays with you. Eventually, it can become transmuted into a kind of

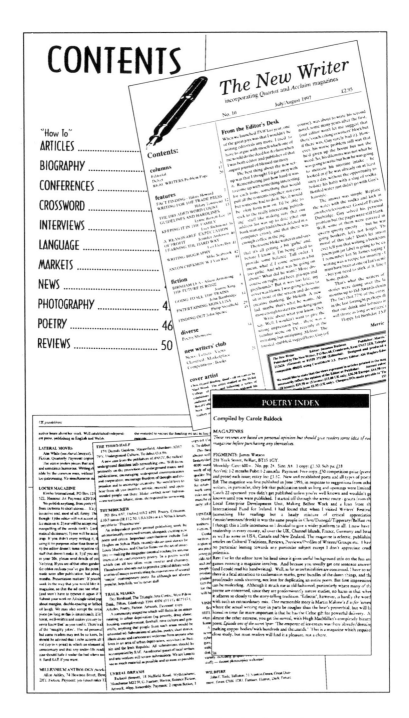

Fig. 5. Finding help through writers' magazines.
(Taken from *The New Writer, Writers' Forum* and *Zene.*)

instinct so that you know that what you are doing is correct, even if the reason for it cannot be recalled. Writing is never purely a natural talent, or so good that a little help won't improve it. Fortunately, there are plenty of places to go, whether to brush up a particular technique or for the grim task of sorting out spelling. The local library has details of the following, where you can obtain prospectuses or programmes:

- night classes
- courses
- writing workshops
- writers' groups.

Or you can teach yourself (see Further Reading) through:

- books
- writing magazines
- correspondence courses.

Taking it further
Other areas of study include specific disciplines:

- form (poetry)
- characterisation (short stories)
- plot (novel)
- structure (non-fiction).

You could then go on to specialist skills, like researching background material.

SPEAKING VOLUMES

It has been suggested that all writers need to read ten times as much as they write.

The essential bookshelf
Reference books are a necessity:

- dictionary
- thesaurus
- encyclopaedia
- handbooks/manuals on writing
- literary criticism.

Even selecting a dictionary is no simple task:

1. How up-to-date is it?
2. Should it include fairly obscure words (if historical genres are a priority)?
3. Any extras: appendices; quotations; abbreviations; lists of personal names?
4. Are the definitions sufficiently detailed?
5. Are derivations fully explained?

Take into consideration such practicalities as the size of print; if difficult to read, it will put you off looking things up. Good, thick paper should ensure books stay in decent condition, but check they aren't too cumbersome.

Setting up a library

A good start to a writer's library is with either a copy of the *Writers' & Artists' Yearbook* (*WAY*), or *The Writer's Handbook* (*WH*). Commonly thought of as directories of publications, both contain plenty of useful details, although feature material formerly in the *WH* is now contained in a separate volume *The Writer's Companion*. *WAY* covers most areas of interest to all kinds of writers, such as **Public Lending Right** for which all authors should register in order to receive a minute fee every time a copy of their book is borrowed from a library. (See Useful Addresses.) *WAY* also ranges from the basics about submitting your work to the complexities of **copyright**, **libel**, **tax** and so on.

Suzanne Ruthven's book *From an Editor's Desk*, in itself invaluable, provides a comprehensive list of all the books likely to prove useful to the writer, as do most books on writing. You can borrow library books to assess which are going to be indispensable, and most writing magazines include reviews of books about writing; there are innumerable titles, for beginners and experts, from the general to the specific. Writers sometimes disagree on certain areas, so read around to make up your own mind. Celia Brayfield clearly knows what she is talking about in her excellent book, *Bestseller: secrets of successful writing*, as does Valerie Blumenthal, whose series about writing a novel appeared in *The New Writer*.

INVESTING IN TECHNOLOGY

Many writers feel they cannot be truly creative unless they have a pen in their hand, at least to start with. Only then are poems, stories and novels word-processed. Non-fiction, too, may come to life in

1. If buying secondhand printer and computer separately, are they compatible?

2. Make sure you get the manuals for each of them – and the phone numbers of reliable companies for back-up.

3. Shop around for disks, ink cartridges, refills and so on. Are they easy to track down? Expensive?

4. What about spare parts? Find out the nearest reliable computer company.

5. Has the computer ample memory? Find out the best way to keep your files in order. Get in the habit of copying everything important to disk and deleting what's no longer required.

6. If you don't know how to touch-type, have a suitable programme installed and practise – saves lots of time in the long-run.

7. Experiment with desktop publishing or just typescripts and layout. Once you've chosen the most suitable for correspondence, stick to it. Don't use something different on every single letter.

8. Does the spell-check facility include a dictionary and thesaurus? Remember the spell-check will pass 'wrong' words such as 'these' instead of 'those'.

9. If the word-count only applies to the entire document, block the piece you need to check and copy onto a temporary new file.

10. Remember, computers are not as logical as they're cracked up to be. Don't panic if something goes wrong: cursor vanishes; mouse freezes; printer starts squeaking. Switch off and start all over again.

Fig. 6. Checklist for computer requirements,
or how to live in peace with your pc.

longhand, although it is possible to sit in front of a screen and merrily type away until you've knocked out that day's 15,000 words (or 1,500). As long as what you write is for your benefit, you need nothing more elaborate than a pen, but when the time comes to communicate, a more suitable means will be necessary.

Choosing your technology
Typewriter or computer? The very thought of either may horrify you; at worst, they are both infuriating. Typewriters are cheaper, portable, far easier to get the hang of but noisier and much more time-consuming. Computers can be very expensive and very complicated, but they have a starring role in this technological

age. Once you get to know them, you won't know yourself, since they have far more uses, including:

- word count
- spellcheck
- as many copies as you want at the touch of a button
- desktop publishing
- databases
- spreadsheets
- mailshots.

It is possible to teach yourself to use a computer, even though all manuals seem to be written in a foreign language. For most of us who start off convinced it's a necessary evil, going on a course or night class is the quickest way to learn about keeping up with the Jones's, or whatever the latest model is called. One other essential: get to know somebody who lives and breathes computers, and will happily play with yours for hours when it goes wrong. If a computer can go wrong, it will.

Living in peace with your pc

It would be a mistake to claim that familiarity breeds contempt where computers are concerned, but you can learn to get along with them. Even after several years, you'll still recall when you first sat down in front of that blank, forbidding screen, disk clenched in trembling fingers, utterly convinced that touching 'enter' meant pressing the Red Button and the End of the World as we know it. Fortunately, no matter how annoying computers can be (particularly when forgetting to save the last hour's work or making you decide to delete a file which turns out to be absolutely vital 24 hours later), you will soon regard it as an essential.

Stocking up on other overheads

Writing needn't be a very expensive hobby but costs can mount up. It does look more professional, particularly when first contacting a publication, if you send your mail first class (as well as making sure it arrives). Second class post is fine for less urgent post, such as SAEs and reminders. Other than stamps, the main expense is likely to be purchasing books, but you also need to lay in supplies of stationery:

- pens and pencils
- rubbers, paperclips
- sellotape and scissors

- notebooks
- A4 paper
- envelopes.

Pens are notorious for disappearing, even with one in every room as well as by the phone; you never know when inspiration may strike. It's useful to have blue as well as black, to differentiate your notes or for corrections, if red ink reminds you of school. With A4 notebooks, the number of words per page is roughly equivalent to one page on the computer, depending on the size of your writing. 'Reporter's' notebooks are a handy size, or something smaller to carry around in case of bright ideas, with another for noting expenses and sales.

Choosing the right paper

You could devise headed paper yourself on the computer. You can also do compliments slips: about four to a sheet gives a decent sized space, but they need cutting with a guillotine unless you have a straight eye. A4 paper, *ie* typing or copier paper, is available in packets of 500 sheets.

Heavier paper is often recommended, but that means fewer sheets per envelope and more postage. If the contents are going to be a tight fit, fold each sheet twice and use an A5 envelope. To prevent anything being squashed, stiffen an A4 envelope with a piece of thin cardboard and write in capitals along the bottom: 'Please do not bend'. This size can also be used for parcels or, if you've had books delivered, recycle the packaging; it's common practice to re-use envelopes, particularly in the Small Press world, and more environmentally sound than double-spacing on one side of A4. Window envelopes save time when sending out post and you may also be able to print out SAEs on the computer, making the envelopes look more business-like.

CASE STUDIES

Dexter gets a sense of place

Dexter has got writer's block (not to mention cramp) from sitting in a corner of a small sofa, trying to jot down ideas for poems. Shelley-Danielle can't bear to be parted from him, but she really doesn't want to miss her TV programmes either. Fortunately, although it's not a huge flat, they hardly ever use the tiny dining room, so perhaps he could work in there for an hour or so? Shelley-Danielle has an even better idea – she'll get it redecorated so he'll have just a perfect den. She starts making plans and designs, and changing her mind, but still calls the decorators in. Dexter retreats to the sofa.

Brent is in the wrong place

The last review copy Brent requested was accompanied by promotional merchandise, including a huge wall chart. He can only fill it in by spreading it on the floor.

Of course, he won't be writing down the interviews and press calls, press nights and private views in a variety of colours – just in his best handwriting and, in the case of the well-known movie star he's due to interview at the end of the week, in capitals. Had he taken the time to be more organised, though, he might have seen there wasn't much space for including details of the book launch he'd agreed to attend – twenty minutes before the interview, at the other end of town.

Katrina discovers there's a time and place for everything

Katrina now knows that computer error is when you realise that buying one was a big mistake. Hers is second-hand, since all she needs is a straightforward word processor, but none of her friendly neighbourhood technophiles can get the printer to work. The computer shop says it has to be re-built at a cost of £400. Her friend's 15-year-old brother says that's because they don't actually know what's wrong but hope it will correct itself during the process. An hour later, he's got the printer up and running.

DISCUSSION POINTS

1. How organised are you? Is there room for an improvement – or are you in danger of taking too much on?

2. What's the best way for you to keep on reading and writing on a regular basis?

3. Do you find you're full of ideas, but it's hard getting them down on paper? Write a list assessing your strengths and weaknesses.

ASSIGNMENT

To make life, and writing, easier draw up a series of lists: timetables (daily, weekly, monthly); books you want to read; basic necessities.

3
Dealing with Finances

The financial aspects of writing need attention right from the start:

- budgeting and calculating expenses
- how to apply for grants and awards
- dealing with tax
- chasing up payment.

BUDGETING AND FORWARD PLANNING

In most professions payment is made in advance or once the job is done. With writing, you can never tell how long you might wait. And few people would work for nothing, no matter how much they love their job. This can be expedient, however, since the small press world often revolves around favours; payment in kind is an investment which will stand you in good stead where your CV and your reputation are concerned.

Scratching a living?

Scales of payments for writers are exceptionally erratic, many amounts apparently chosen on a 'stick-a-pin in it' basis. For example, with some regional papers a 250-word review (all of half-an-hour's work) may be £20, yet a 1,000-word feature is £40. If the latter is an interview, it probably involves travelling, researching the subject, drawing up a list of questions, conducting the interview, then writing it. That said, few readers notice who writes reviews whereas you invariably garner some compliments about the interviews.

Deciding on what you are going to write

Writing non-fiction
Non-fiction is the steadiest means of making a living from writing because there are so many areas to cover and a never-ending demand.

MONTHLY PAYMENTS RECEIVED

2	Journal article	$180
5	News items	£33
5	Sale of *Fiver Guides*	£45.50
12	Entry for reference book	£60
12	Work on book promotion	£200
13	Magazine article	£180
13	Book reviews	£100
15	Short Story Writers Survival Pack	£46
26	Entry for reference book	£60
31	News items	£28
31	Filler for magazine	£10

BREAKDOWN OF ITEMS
(find out about payment in dollars?)
Regular contributions: news items; book reviews
Short-term projects: entries for reference book; book promotion
Sales: booklets and packs
Other: magazine articles; fillers

Fig. 7. Keeping records of payments.

Writing fiction

When it comes to fiction, however, for new authors, it is more a question of prestige than profit. Publishing prose is no guarantee of gainful employment, although women's magazines pay handsomely for short stories. Few publishers bring out collections although, as the editors of *Metropolitan* explained when setting up the magazine, the short story is an ideal form for this busy age. As for novels, some popular writers have earned themselves a small fortune (some an absolutely huge one). When starting out, hang on to the day job and invest in a few lottery tickets.

Writing poetry

Nor is a poet's lot a wealthy one; even the better known rarely make a fortune solely from poems. The money comes from tours, readings, lectures and workshops. Very few publications pay for poetry, although the amount is frequently more than that for prose. As for readings, it's worth doing a bit of travelling around, if the reward is £60 for ten minutes' recitation. There again, you could end up splitting the takings on the door for a somehow unpublicised event: £20 between twelve of you.

Planning ahead

So here you are with an enjoyable hobby, on your bookshelves a pleasing number of publications containing your work, and newsagents occasionally stock a magazine with something of yours in. It's wonderful to see your name in print, and even better seeing the odd cheque going into your account. If you plan to continue having more and more work published, now is the time to sort out your finances, while they are still manageable.

APPLYING FOR GRANTS, AWARDS AND SPONSORSHIP

The Arts Council's Arts for Everyone programme and the A4E Express have received a great many applications for 'imaginative and innovative projects of high quality'. Groups on the mailing list are kept informed by the Regional Arts Boards (RABs), automatically receiving newsletters and press releases; individuals need to be on the database in some capacity or other (*eg* as a writer who can provide a service, such as running workshops). Though opportunities for individuals are limited, few writers work entirely in isolation. You can get involved with others to some extent, perhaps as part of a writers' group or working with a publisher, which enables you to find out more about grants. Some criteria are particularly stringent, however.

Both *WH* and *WAY* contain sections on bursaries, fellowships, grants and prizes. The latter will usually have some press coverage when they are awarded so keep an eye out for newspaper reports. Most art grants have priorities of some kind, depending on:

- financial status
- place
- age
- genre.

There are grants to cover all kinds of writing and all kinds of writers:

– The Paul Hamlyn Foundation for poets with one published collection or one accepted for publication.

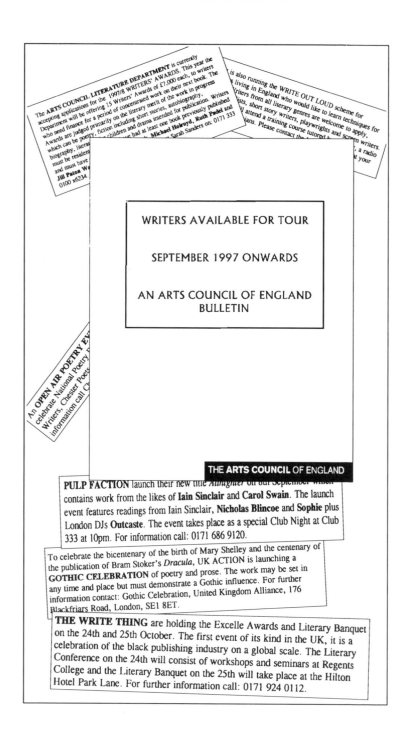

Fig. 8. Finding information about grants, awards and events.

– The Encore Award, Society of Authors, for a second novel.

– Tom-Gallon Trust, biennial award, also made by the Society of Authors to fiction writers of limited means who have had at least one short story accepted.

– The Economist/Richard Casement Internship, for journalists aged under 24; three months writing about science and technology.

Acquiring business skills

Grants are not simply for the creative process. If you decide to turn your hobby into a career as a self-employed freelance, in effect you are running a small business. You then need to acquire new skills, for which there are many different kinds of training programmes, some reasonably cheap or even free:

- marketing
- research
- running workshops
- presentation skills
- fundraising
- self-publishing
- getting on with the Internet.

CALCULATING EXPENSES

Asking for receipts for each piece of photocopying, every stamp, may seem like nit-picking, but that's what's expected of you for tax purposes and pence soon grow into pounds. Every purchase should be entered up, and the corresponding receipts kept for each quarter or each month. Stationery alone soon adds up if you have a lot of correspondence. Travel isn't cheap either, whether it's trips to the city library for research, or the theatre to review a play. Books or magazines purchased for research can be costly, as can subscriptions: magazines, societies or organisations. Arrange for a breakdown of your telephone bill so you can keep an eye on business calls; if you are doing enough writing to be described as self-employed, a proportion of your household costs, such as heating, is allowable.

Adding it all up

Check with every outlet if you are entitled to expenses; some

SAMPLE OF MONTHLY EXPENSES

POSTAGE AND STATIONERY

1st	Stamps	£0.82
3rd	"	£4.45
4th	Typing paper	£3.99
6th	New ink cartridge	£19.99
10th	Photocopying	£1.05
10th	Package	£6.31
11th	Collecting fax	£1.00
12th	Envelopes	£1.29

BREAKDOWN

Letters received (including books): 133
Letters posted: 98, including 7 enquiries – 2 replies so far

OTHER

13th	New dictionary	£12.99
20th	Magazine subs	£18

EXPENSES TO BE CLAIMED

Phone calls (publisher; distributor; magazines; radio):24	£9.60
Packages (copy of magazine)	£2.41
Letters: 19	£15.20
Press releases: 33	£13.20
Photocopying: 17 @ 5p	£0.85

Fig. 9. Expenses calculation.

publications are prepared to cover this even if they don't make payments for your work. Working out exactly what you are owed to cover your outlay takes a lot of doing, but when you add it all up you'll see that it's worth it. So is adding up the month's cheques – usually as gratifying as updating your CV.

Keeping records
Always keep a record of your work for each category: poetry, non-fiction and so on:

- title and nature of piece
- where and when it was submitted

- outcome of submission
- if accepted, amount of payment.

Prioritise outlets, particularly the most promising. Some may be very friendly but difficult to contact; others extremely efficient, except when it comes to payment. Even if a small fortune is 'in the post', don't bank on it. Try to ensure you have enough money to prevent any cash flow problems. Like buses, cheques tend to come along in threes, when they do turn up. Then there's no sign of any for ages.

TAXING PROBLEMS

Tax returns fill all of us with horror, but help is available. *Starting your own business?* is a useful booklet (ref: CWL 1) from the Inland Revenue or the National Insurance Contributions Agency which tells you everything you thought you would never get the hang of to do with tax and National Insurance contributions. Tax is one topic which often crops up in writing magazines and there's invariably a chapter on the subject in writing books.

Even when your earnings are a long way under the personal allowance, you still have to complete tax returns. Remember that you need to keep all tax records for six years. A turnover of less than £15,000 means that simple tax accounts are all that's required; once you're earning more than that, you'll probably be employing an accountant anyway.

Filling in forms

Freelance writing being so erratic when it comes to payment, officialdom often finds it impossible to comprehend that it is equally impossible for you to provide an accurate estimate of future earnings. Be prepared for their reactions to your earnings, ranging from outright surprise to suspicion that anyone can manage on such a low amount. Some officials are flatteringly impressed, then starting telling you about the novel they were always going to write, if they didn't have to earn a living.

As well as calculating tax returns, you may have to sort out several sets of figures, for various organisations, for different periods: council tax; Family Credit; student grants. Family Credit is twice a year, grants crop up each term. Form-filling is numbingly dull but gets easier with practice; it's important to adopt the habit of keeping a stringent check on all documents and to keep copies. In the early stages of a writing career, all you need to do is submit a declaration stating that the figures quoted show your earnings and expenses over the past twelve months.

National Insurance Contributions
If you are aged 16 or over and self-employed (full- or part-time), you must pay a weekly flat rate Class 2 contribution. If net earnings for the previous year are less than £3,500, and unlikely to exceed that amount in the coming year, you can apply for a certificate of exception.

You still have to advise whether you want to pay voluntary contributions; you may wish to pay Class 2 contributions so that you are entitled to the various benefits such as retirement pension or incapacity benefit.

CHECKING THE PAYMENT IS IN THE POST

Most writers are amateurs, in the true sense of the word. Payment may initially seem like the icing on the cake. When writing as a hobby, seeing your name in print is often reward enough, but even if you are doing something you love *and* getting paid for it, always be professional when it comes to finances.

Submitting invoices
Rarely necessary for poetry or prose, invoices are not always essential for non-fiction either. They can be particularly useful, though, if in doubt as to the amount of payment when something is accepted 'on spec', *ie* you wrote with suggestions to a magazine and the editor asked to see some of your work. The simple solution is to enquire whether an invoice is required. Where payment is negotiable, if an invoice is required the editor will have to inform you of the amount due so the form is correctly completed. Remember 'negotiable' means just that. This is where your command of the English language comes into its own: gently insisting on a decent rate of payment without falling out with the editor altogether.

The **cover sheet** usually acts as an invoice and is forwarded to the accounts department. Standard invoices tend to be a small, flimsy sheet of paper, but at least provide a record – indeed, a pleasant aide memoire to flick through, noting all the sales. You can cheer yourself up when one of the daily papers turns down that sure-fire interview.

Getting hold of your money

If entitled to payment, you are equally entitled to receive it promptly. Admittedly, when dealing with the small press writers make allowances for delays as their financial problems are well known. Problems can also crop up in organisations where the phrase 'cash flow' conjures up the image of a cornucopia. Some publications have an accounts department where, to put it in musical terms, they don't know their Mozart from their Elgar.

Avoid blaming the editor for late payments. If you want to stay on good terms, try and enlist their help in tracking down that elusive cheque, rather than ringing up and playing hell. In one particular magazine, allegedly, the accounts person used to go in once a fortnight and whatever didn't get done within a couple of hours was left until the next time. Letters went unanswered, phone calls were never returned, but one letter to the editor did the trick and the cheque duly arrived. Do your best to remain cool and calm, and you should collect. Patience is useful when you finally get hold of the right person in the accounts department because, far from apologising, they're likely to airily give the impression that they are putting themselves out to do you a huge favour.

Resorting to desperate measures

All writers have horror stories where payments are concerned, particularly when involved with publications which end up owing them hundreds of pounds. Once may look like carelessness, twice, or even more, is sadly not uncommon. The main problem, as with all businesses, is that no organisation can afford to let anyone think they are in deep trouble. Writing is more vulnerable than other professions because so much of it is done in advance. If a week in politics is a long time, it can be even longer in publishing.

If your article doesn't appear, at least it can often be re-vamped and angled to suit another magazine. However, it's hard to be philosophical if you are a regular contributor, due payment of hundreds of pounds for several items. Worse still some writers, convinced they've cracked it with their own series, for example, give up the day job. If the publisher goes bankrupt, there's not a lot you can do about it.

Finding friends in need

The whole process of chasing up payment is time-consuming and frustrating. You need to take a big breath and be determined to stand up for yourself. The easy way out is to decide to chalk it up to experience. There is a tendency to get a bit paranoid, convinced you're the only contributor who hasn't been paid; other people don't have these problems. But they do, and they always will if the villain of the piece is allowed to get away with it. Fortunately, amongst the other advantages of joining such an organisation, you can turn to these groups for advice and support, or to bring a little pressure to bear:

- National Union of Journalists
- Society of Authors
- Society of Women Writers and Journalists
- Women Writers Network.

Chasing up payment

Having submitted your work, with an invoice, it's been published quite some time ago, the cheque still hasn't arrived. Now what?

- Infuriating scenario no. 1: Every time you ring/write, no response.
- No. 2: 'Cross their heart and hope to die', the cheque is in the post.

Now you must decide whether you can afford to lose any chance of more work. If there have already been problems, ask yourself if you want to go through this rigmarole every single time. You could also make a few direct enquiries, to see what other contributors think about the situation.

Once you decide to insist on payment, keep up the momentum and keep in contact with them.

They may pay up, simply to get rid of you, but don't let it drag on indefinitely. Choose a realistic deadline, perhaps a month hence, then send a polite letter enclosing an invoice in case the original 'has gone missing' and warning that if payment is not received by a certain date, you will take steps to recover the debt by:

1.   Informing one of the societies listed above.

2.   Consulting a writing magazine.

3.   Taking legal advice or finding out about Small Claims Court
     procedure.

This is meant to be the letter which does the trick, and probably
does nine times out of ten, but it all depends who you're dealing
with. The 'last resort' letter is doomed to failure when you come up
against somebody who is either exceptionally hard-faced or
incredibly naïve. The former will call your bluff whilst the latter
adopts an ostrich attitude, completely ignoring the problem in the
hope it will go away. Nevertheless, a week before the deadline, send
a final warning. Then carry out exactly what you said you would do.

Once you start trying to recover your money, it is important to be
aware what's involved and how far you may have to go, such as to
court. It's best to be prepared for the fact that you could have a fight
on your hands. But you're not the villain of the piece, and justice
should be done for the sake of all writers who are likely to end up
out of pocket.

CASE STUDIES

Dexter settles things once and for all
Dexter occasionally provides film reviews for a specialist magazine.
They advise him of a change of editor, but don't inform him of a
change of policy until he's submitted two lots of work. As recent
copies of the magazine have not been sent to him, he is unaware that
the new editor has not been using his work. Shelley-Danielle decides
this is a job for his agent and writes a lengthy letter on his behalf,
insisting on payment, otherwise it's the Small Claims Court. The
magazine pays up but the cheque is accompanied by a letter bluntly
warning him that he won't get any more work with that publication,
nor any others in the same line of business.

Brent settles out of court
Brent is asked to cover a prestigious annual arts festival. It's a lot of
time and effort, with complicated arrangements, including travel, so
that he can see as many events as possible. He's being paid a fair
amount for his trouble... until the magazine goes bust. Each time
he writes or rings the editor swears blind that he is sending the
cheque; even that fail-safe, the Small Claims Court, has no effect.
Brent decides to have it out face-to-face with the editor, and he does
come home with payment of a kind: a state-of-the-art midi system.
A month later, only the radio works properly.

Katrina settles an argument

Katrina suggests to the editor of a lifestyle magazine that it may be eligible for an annual award. The deadline is imminent and he can't see the point of going to all that trouble when they're hardly likely to win anyway, but she still gets an application form. As the magazine could be said to provide training in journalism and graphic design for young people (though said young people refer to it as slave labour), the form is sent in. The magazine makes the short-list and the editor and deputy are invited to the award ceremony. Even though it doesn't win, as Katrina points out a nomination for a prestigious award is good publicity, worth mentioning on the cover and in advertising.

DISCUSSION POINTS

1. Do you have a good head for figures? If not, do you know somebody who has, or is it something you feel it would be a good idea to learn about?

2. Form-filling is a necessary evil; what's the best way for you to keep your accounts?

3. Do you have a way with words? Practice makes perfect, particularly with letters asking for payment and reminders.

ASSIGNMENT

Having decided what areas of writing are for you, read up about the various awards, prizes and so on. These are so diverse, it's well worth investigating – it could be you!

4
Marketing Yourself and Your Work

Marketing is next to writing itself in importance, and involves the following:

- Understanding promotion and publicity.
- Making the most of networking.
- Using your CV for promotional purposes, such as contacting editors.
- Learning how to deal with rejection.

MAKING A NAME FOR YOURSELF AND YOUR WORK

Unfortunately, most people are convinced that marketing is the art of talking people into buying things they really don't need. Writers especially tend to feel their business is purely creative, nothing to do with anything commercialised. They have faith in the old saying: 'If a man build a better mouse-trap than his neighbour, though he live in a wood, the world will beat a path to his door.' In fact, the world pays absolutely *no* attention whatsoever, unless said inventor puts up signs saying something like: 'First class mouse-trap – this way' or, 'Buy one, get one free'.

Promotion and publicity

If people are not made aware of your talent for writing, they will never find out. *That* is the art of marketing. As with all the arts, somebody who learns how to write competently and understands about marketing will always succeed far more than the tortured genius languishing in an attic.

> **From the moment inspiration first strikes, marketing goes hand in hand with the actual piece of work.**

For most editors or writers it comes first: do your market research, locate a gap in the market, write a piece to fill it, submit it, sit back, wait for the cheque. Of course it's not that easy, but it isn't difficult either, because from the first piece of published work you are part of a **network**.

NETWORKING

Making contact/keeping in contact with others with whom you have a common interest is invaluable for marketing. Even an isolated creature like a writer has ample opportunities for networking with others, especially if they have a day job involving a more lucrative side of writing (like tuition) and may come in contact with:

- fellow contributors/other writers: novelists, poets, journalists, reviewers
- editors
- organisers and publicists (events, conferences, writers' groups)
- publishers.

Sometimes correspondence seems to take as much time as your writing, but it saves a lot of hard work when you go on to produce more substantial work, such as books, since you won't have to 'cold-call' editors praying that they'll take a chance on the unknown.

Make a name for yourself first by having your work published as widely as possible, collaborate with others (for example, reviewing their books), and you'll find people willing to co-operate, and a receptive audience. It's also useful to have your name on mailing lists, particularly of publishers, organisers and publicists.

Mailing lists

This is your record of the names and addresses of contacts, plus some which could prove useful, such as promising new outlets. You automatically receive updated information, and build up your own list. Then when the time comes for you to do some promotion, such as issuing press releases, all the details are to hand.

LIAISING WITH THE ARTS COUNCIL AND REGIONAL ARTS BOARD

Most of your work, especially books, should sell well locally. That means not just in your birthplace, but the whole of the county and

Freelance Market News

An essential guide for freelance writers · Established 1968

NEW MARKETS

EDITOR'S DESK

Thank you to everyone who entered our Travel Article Competition. It proved to be our most popular competition so far.

...anted for a top-...rested should ...ed, Glenthorne ...ton W6 OLG.

...en relaunched ...r **Knowledge**, ...covering those ...cient sciences, ...g gap between ...The first edition ...the planets, ...teries of Egypt. ...disc. ...P.O.

Vol 3 · No 3

WRITERS NEWS

JANUARY 1997

BBC scouts for new talent

by Richard Morris, Studio Correspondent

For love of ...

Contents

MONTHLY · VOL. 1 No. 2 · JUNE 1997 · £2.00

WRITERS' BULLETIN

ISSN 1368-5392

EDITORIAL

What an amazing response! Thank you all for your kind words and good wishes for the future of Writers' Bulletin. I hope our endeavours will justify your praise. It has to be said that we didn't realise how many new friends we would make while compiling the information for these pages – most gratifying.

As we progress with making new contacts and refining the ways in which information is presented, we hope to make our new baby even better value for money; carry a wide range of markets and resources, festivals and conferences. Chris and I will be attending as many events as possible, both to publicise Writers' Bulletin and make new friends in the publishing world. I hope to meet lots of our readers at these events too, in order to find out what you like (and dislike) about WB so that we can make it the best markets magazine in the country – if not the world.

Meanwhile, if you have any comments, anecdotes, gripes or plaudits you wish to air, please write to us. Cheers,

John

In this issue

SUBSCRIPTION RATES (10 issues)
UK: £20 pa
EC: £22 pa (airmail)
Rest of World: £30 pa (airmail)
Please make cheque payable to Writers' Bulletin

Edited, published and produced by Chris McCallum and John Barton.
All correspondence to Chris at PO BOX 86, Altrincham, Cheshire WA14 2LN.
Please enclose an SAE for replies.

Fig. 10. Writers' magazines.
(Taken from *Writers' Bulletin, Writers News* and *Freelance Market News*.)

perhaps further still, throughout the area covered by the Regional Arts Board (RAB). They should already have your details in their Writers' Directory and Web site, especially if you consider the following possibilities:

1. Running a workshop or a course.
2. Operating an appraisal service.
3. Making yourself available to work in schools.

As well as possible outlets, there is a better than average chance of selling books when people have had a chance to get to know you from:

- different publications
- performances in various venues
- working with you for several organisations.

Utilising the Regional Arts Board

You should also keep a list of local events, from tourism to literary matters. Get to know the organisers of any festivals in the vicinity. Contact them as soon as it's over, so that you have a better chance of getting involved in next year's. The RAB may include a review of your book in their newsletter and keep a copy in their library. They can also provide you with a press list, to assist your mail-out.

Utilising the Arts Council

Similarly, send details to the Arts Council for inclusion in their quarterly bulletin, *Writers Available for Tour*. As well as these details, it includes notes, news and a diary. The Arts Council also provides a list of writers' groups nationwide, though the one maintained by the RABs is more up-to-date, as is Jill Dick's *Directory of Writers' Circles* (see Further Reading). The Arts Council Staff List has details of all RABs, so you can send them press releases, particularly in places where you once lived, worked or studied. Even a link as simple as this may interest the local paper.

PROMOTING YOURSELF: THE CV

The **curriculum vitae** now seems to assume as much importance as a birth certificate, judging by the number of advertisements for preparing them. They are usually described as **CV**s. CVs serve two main purposes: to inform future employers of your abilities and a

CV 1993–97

Carole Baldock
52 Dorrell Park, Hackney Bridge, London SE19 6XJ: 0123 456 7892
BA Hons Librarianship & Information Technology. Freelance Writer

Publications
How To Books (foreword by Jimmy Mulville): *Writing Reviews: How to Write about Arts and Leisure for Pleasure and Profit.*
Knight & Bishop: Information Packs: *GCSE Literature Guides; Teenage Pregnancy; Bullying; Money Management for Teenagers.*
Cherrybite Publications: *Fiver Guides writers' directories.*
The Writer's Survival Pack: short stories; poetry; non-fiction.

Book Proposals
Sheldon Press: *How to Succeed as a Single Parent.*
Contributor: *Children's Britannica.*
Routledge: *Encyclopaedia of Contemporary British Culture.*

Marketing, Publishing and Promotion
Spike Small Press (Partner); *Fidelio; Author-Publisher Network.*
Performance poet and publicist: The Dead Good Poets' Society.

Appraisals/Critiques; Teaching
Cheshire County Council's MSS Appraisal Scheme.
Commonword Ltd's Appraisal Service (Manchester)
1992 MAWW Workshop: Writing for Different Markets.
1993 Lecture (John Moores University): Technical/Creative Writing.

Editing:
Books Editor: *Event* (*Liverpool Post & Echo* listings magazine); *Theatre Magazine.*
Associate Editor: *Orbis* (an international quarterly of poetry and prose).

Regular Contributor
News, reviews, features, interviews: *Writers News; Freelance Market News; The Writers' Club; The New Writer.* Column: *Lateral Moves.* Series: *Writers' Forum; Writers' Guide.*

Articles
Assistant Librarian: Cap and gown . . .cap in hand
Library Management: Marketing the libraries
Ms London: Funny things – Women
The Scotsman: Single Minded (Mother's Day feature)
Manchester Evening News: Reading Volumes (book reviews)
Big Issue NW: Interview with Lily Savage.

Other Work Commissioned
Articles, features, interviews (education, books, art, theatre, music, film, restaurants): *tate; Art Monthly; National Trust Magazine; Parents & Computers; So; The Western Mail; Boys First; Young People Now; Youth Clubs Magazine; The New Internationalist*
USA: *Calliope* and *Faces* (Simon & Schuster Education Group); Canada: *Writers' Block.*

Fig. 11. Sample CV.

record of your achievements (your writing history). One business-man apparently derives great comfort at times of stress by perusing his CV, all thirty-six pages of it, although as is often the case with writing less is best. 'Keep it simple' is a tried and tested formula. A one-page CV should suffice and having to concentrate your accomplishments into that space means including only the best.

> **Relevance is what counts, not showing off.**

The editor of a poetry magazine is not interested in learning that you are about to start your novel, any day now. Should he be a devoted fan of Wilfred Owen, however, and your book is based on the discovery of new information about the poet, as an expert, his advice would be invaluable.

Categorising your CV

For those who turn their hand to various markets, it's useful to have a CV for each one rather than trying to cram everything in, whilst also maintaining a master copy. When you want to impress some VIP, a mini version can be incorporated in your covering letter, along with basic background information about educational qualifications. Again, even if you've done marvellously well in certain areas, unless it's applicable leave it out. Editors are expert at skimming paperwork; they do not meander over every single word.

As regards personal details, one excellent piece of information handed out at university was to leave these to the very end – including your age, gender and address. It's just a precaution, which should not be necessary, but even in these enlightened times any or all of these can put somebody off from the start.

A good start is to categorise your work, beginning with the most important (*ie* relevant) information, usually any books you've had published. It's reasonable to assume that you are therefore capable of any kind of writing. Other areas may include:

- editing
- teaching (workshops, lectures)
- reviewing; providing appraisals
- articles
- competition prizes and awards.

Having work on file

When submitting articles, mention in your CV whether you are a regular contributor, write a column or a series. Include work commissioned, particularly if your *pièce de résistance* has been chosen by an annual journal or is on file at a prestigious publication. **On file** is a kind of limbo; it's easy to conclude that your writing is good but not good enough. There are many reasons for work to be retained on file, and not being good enough isn't one of them. More likely, it's a question of space or theme, or else something similar has recently been used.

Curiously, on the very rare occasions the files are re-opened, your services tend to be urgently required. Although it's nearly as infuriating to be expected to drop everything to help out with a project for a company that hasn't been in touch for as long as twelve months, it can prove to be a golden opportunity. Freelances learn to expect the unexpected.

Promoting your work

When you first start writing, a CV may strike you as somewhat pointless but it soon starts building up. Well-known writer Alison Chisholm lives up to her own advice: make your goal making a name for yourself. Once work has been published in one magazine it encourages you to approach others and should lead on to success in other areas.

There is a danger of falling between two stools when it comes to self-promotion: false modesty and blowing your own trumpet. Playing down your achievements is pointless if you wish to succeed as a writer, but don't make a meal out of every single thing. Concentrate on your best work and make the most of it; you have to sell yourself as well as your writing so never sell yourself short, but stick to the edited highlights rather than adding up every publication anything of yours has ever appeared in. Even if it is a considerable amount, it suggests you have nothing better to do. The faintest hint of desperation about anything never bodes well for anyone, especially writers.

INTRODUCING YOURSELF TO EDITORS

To paraphrase a popular song: why can't an editor be more like a writer? How much easier life would be if editors really understood what a struggle it is for writers – and if writers had the vaguest idea of what's involved in being an editor. Writers often don't realise how much work is involved in editing, though they might suspect it's an onerous occupation, judging by the length of time replies can take. Approaching an editor should be done with great care, to get into their good books. One poetry magazine receives more submissions in a week than it publishes in a year, while another editor reckons that only two per cent of the work sent in matches his requirements.

Creating a good impression

An editor can already tell a great deal by looking at your envelope:

- far too small: obviously not even room to include the SAE
- far too big: what on earth are they expecting in return?
- yellow with age: is their work likely to be fresh and original?
- brightly coloured, with a giraffe peering coyly over the top: funny peculiar?

And it doesn't take a graphologist to know that handwriting is a give-away. Make sure it isn't:

- indecipherable
- misspelt
- badly presented, such as so high up the envelope it's almost obliterated by the postmark
- too faint.

It's even possible to tell a person's age from the handwriting since older people tend to have a much fairer hand. Younger writers often produce something fancier, with the aid of a computer.

Submitting work

Never submit anything unless you've actually read the magazine in question. Better still several issues, all of them analysed so thoroughly you virtually know them off by heart, though not on the basis that flattery will get you everywhere ('I'm writing to say how *very, very much* I enjoyed your simply wonderful magazine'). It's market research which does that; without it, you'll get nowhere.

For submissions on disk, save your work in a text file (ASCII), in case of computer incompatibility. Always include the hard copy, *ie* a printed version, and stick to the basic rules of presentation when submitting work:

- one side only of each sheet of A4 paper
- double-spaced

- wide margins all round
- each page numbered
- neatly typed or word-processed, in a clear typescript in a large enough point size
- The End typed on the last page, together with your name and address
- separate sheets held together by a paperclip or enclosed in a thin plastic folder.

Be warned, getting this last one wrong can spell disaster. Editors' views on the various fastenings are apt to be idiosyncratic, such as a loathing for coloured paperclips. If an editor does have strong feelings on this (or any other) subject, it will be spelled out in the contributors' guidelines, one reason why requesting them is a good first move. It is also recommended that all submissions (other than books) be accompanied by a cover sheet, bearing the following:

- name and address
- title
- word count
- details of any illustrations.

First British Serial Rights
Bearing in mind the saying 'Just because you're paranoid doesn't mean they're not after you', writers are advised to add **First British Serial Rights**. Serial, even if it's just a short article? In this instance the word relates to anything published on a regular basis, such as a series of issues. This shows that the work has not been published before, and gives the right to publish it for the first time and once only in Britain. You can then sell the work anywhere in the world, other than Britain, but if the publisher wishes to use it again they must pay you once more. If any question arises about the sale of your rights, get expert advice before signing anything.

Ringing or writing?
Opinion is split, but whatever you decide always check the name of the person you wish to contact and keep that initial call short and sweet so they're delighted to make your acquaintance. If you need to ring for more information, it may be a good opportunity to see whether the editor is free to talk, just as letters are more useful when sending cuttings or your proposal is a little more complex. The easiest way to decide on your approach depends on which method is

more comfortable; some of us are born letter writers, others are blessed with a telephone manner which could sell a florist's to a hay fever sufferer. As time goes by, these skills, like all the others you acquire as a writer, will improve.

Sending reminders

In an ideal world all letters should receive some kind of response, and reasonably promptly too. But no matter how infuriated you are, think of yourself as setting an example or displaying exquisite courtesy, by following up enquiry letters with a polite reminder. Try to refrain from cynical thoughts about the amount of mail which goes missing in the post. Three times to one particular newspaper. Allegedly.

There's no hard and fast rule about when to send reminders, especially where non-fiction is concerned and the subject is topical, but – not too soon and not too many. Some writing books suggest three months for weekly and monthly publications, six months for quarterlies, though by then it's like being back to square one, approaching the editor for the first time. Where a publication doesn't advise on reply time (*Story Cellar*, for example, say three months), it's probably as well to wait at least six to eight weeks. After all, when you yourself are up to your eyes, how many of your reminders go out on time anyway?

COPING WITH REJECTION

Nobody goes through life without being rejected at some point. It's devastating, sweeping you to the depths of despair, whether you have failed a vital exam or seen the former love of your life having the time of his life with somebody else. It's the crushing disappointment of realising that you've missed a golden opportunity that will never come again.

Hang on a minute. This is an occupation, not life itself, and everybody has suffered like this. It's just how we initially react to rejection. Don't even think that having a piece of writing turned down means that everything you write is rubbish, and you yourself are worthless. Perhaps the main reason rejection is so difficult for writers to deal with is that there can be no closure, to put it in psychological terms: we very rarely know the exact reason for rejection and are therefore unable to rationalise it. The best we can do is decide to accept that there are many reasons why a piece of writing is unsuitable: space, timing, the editor had a bad hair day. It

CAROLE BALDOCK, FREELANCE WRITER: 0123 456 7892
52 DORRELL PARK, HACKNEY BRIDGE, LONDON SE19 6XJ

20th May 199X

Patricia Catkins
Editor, Gerbils are Go!
Precious Pets Publishing Inc.
35 Marryat Avenue
London SR1 9TS

Dear Ms Catkins,

With reference to my previous letter, sent to you with a pre-paid envelope on March 31st, I do not appear to have received any reply.

I look forward to hearing from you.

Yours sincerely,

CAROLE BALDOCK, FREELANCE WRITER: 0123 456 7892
52 DORRELL PARK, HACKNEY BRIDGE, LONDON SE19 6XJ

Patricia Catkins
Editor, Gerbils are Go!
Precious Pets Publishing Inc.
35 Marryat Avenue
London SR1 9TS

Madam,

It's at least three days since I wrote, so why haven't you bothered to reply? You editors, you're all the same, wouldn't know genuine talent if it bit you on the bum.

I'm warning you, Pat, answers on a postcard, by tomorrow noon. Or the hamster gets it.

Yours, in considerable annoyance,

Fig. 12. Sample reminder letters – two different approaches.

is not necessarily because of a poor effort on your part. That said, it's always wise to read your work through very carefully to see if it could be improved.

Even experienced writers are liable to react with irrational thoughts, tempted to ring the editor (or wring the editor's neck) and demand to know *why, why, why*? You may hear cautionary tales about people (and talented ones at that) actually giving up writing because of somebody's criticism. If you are going to take anything that personally, heated kitchens are obviously not the right environment for you. More practical is just to let it go and concentrate on your next piece of work. When one door closes, it often means another opening, giving you time and opportunity for something even better.

CASE STUDIES

Dexter thinks work is child's play

Dexter has a brainwave. While writing poetry he remembers the riddles which used to appear in children's books: 'My first is in donkey, but not in ass...' As puzzles of any kind appear to pay well, and take next to no time to think up, he produces an assortment of half-a-dozen: anagrams, wordsearches and so on. He sends them off to an educational magazine, aimed at children aged 8–14, but doesn't include the solutions to the riddles. The rejection letter is very polite, considering the editor admits that none of the staff could work out the answers.

Brent doesn't realise what he's playing at

Brent is delighted to have some work accepted by a top magazine – only a short piece, but it takes pride of place on his CV. He's not altogether happy with some of the alterations when the proofs arrive – the editor has cut out some of the best jokes – but checks them carefully and sends them back. His feature doesn't appear in the next issue, nor the next. Months go by and he's told it's just a question of space. Then he reads that a new editor has taken over and hastily writes off, to receive a furious reply by return of post. In his rush he never noticed that it was another magazine altogether, with a similar title.

Katrina plays a winning card

Katrina receives a last minute request begging for help, a lot of work for very little money, but it's a subject dear to her heart. So she turns out a good piece of work, delivered on time. Eventually, the editor sends it back, saying it is unsuitable because it is 'too high-brow'. Requests for **kill fees** receive no response. Although it's not exactly professional, Katrina gets it all off her chest to an editor she has known a long time, one who shares her interest and has also had problems with the other outlet. He is very sympathetic and asks to have a look at the piece. Although he doesn't find it quite intellectual enough, after a re-write it is duly published.

DISCUSSION POINTS

1. If what matters most is to see your name in print, how do you plan to research potential markets and make the most of every opportunity to seek publication?

2. Can you monitor your enquiries to different outlets and see if you can improve your acceptance rate?

3. What are the most effective ways for you to deal with having your work turned down?

ASSIGNMENT

Forward planning: decide upon your strategy for the next six months: what work you want to concentrate on and in which areas it is most important for you to make progress.

5
Writing Poetry for Publication

Many people think poetry is the easiest first step in writing. Not necessarily so, as you will discover in this chapter:

- learning all you can about writing poetry
- watching out for the vanity press
- exploring other avenues such as competitions and performance.

READING AND INWARDLY DIGESTING

Love it or hate it, poetry seems to be becoming more and more popular. However, Peter Finch, in his excellent book *The Poetry Business*, half-seriously suggests (quoting Gillian Clarke) 'leaving your mss in a drawer for a few years'. It might be more helpful if fledgling poets tried reading other poets, or even the odd poetry magazine, but in this area above all people appear to be too busy writing to bother with reading.

Setting off as a poet
Traditionally, poets start by having work published in various magazines, working their way up to some of the more prestigious titles. As they become more well-known they are often invited to contribute to anthologies. They can also have their work broadcast, or go in for performance poetry.

Eventually, they garner enough brownie points for a small publisher to suggest a pamphlet of their best work, usually up to about forty pages. If well received, they can approach one of the bigger small presses which publish more substantial collections. Then it's Faber on the phone, followed by Melvyn Bragg desperate for an exclusive interview... Maybe not, yet Tobias Hill had his poems published through the small press, won a *Staple* competition to have a collection printed and now, at 27, has had a book of short stories published by Faber.

Faber is the publisher many poets see as the Holy Grail, and they're on the receiving end of much work from novices who believe in starting at the top. Few of the main publishing houses publish more than one collection a year, as you will see from some basic market research round your local bookstore, but a number of smaller publishers are renowned for poetry. These include Bloodaxe, Carcanet and Seren.

Crafting poetry

If the urge to write poetry comes upon you, there is nothing to do but put pen to paper. Should a similar urge impel you to post your efforts off right, left and centre, pause for a moment. Procrastination may be the thief of time but it does writers a favour. Editors sigh very heavily when informed by some eager beaver that they were inspired to write a poem in ten minutes. The belief that any form of editing fatally interferes with the creative process is about as daft as attempting a new recipe without consulting a cookery book.

Writing is a craft, something you can learn to do – and do well – making it as good as it can possibly be.

If you want to be proud of your work, you must be prepared to put in the time to do justice to it.

Be wary, though, of Rimbaud's comment about poems never being completed, only abandoned; some writers agonise interminably over *le mot juste*. The problem arises because there are so many words to choose from, each with infinite interpretations. Knowing when to stop, once your work is sufficiently polished, becomes instinctive, though you should never let yourself become complacent. Allow, too, for the fact that every reader perceives a poem differently.

Learning from example

The best way to learn? From a poet whose work you admire, either directly by being taught, or indirectly by teaching yourself through reading. It's astonishing how some writers virtually boast about never reading anything, claiming they don't wish to come under the influence of others. That's how they manage to miss warnings about the vanity press.

LEARNING MORE, LOCALLY AND NATIONALLY

The local press and the library have information about events, courses or workshops which give you an opportunity to meet with others of a similar inclination.

For those less gregarious, a better route may be the small press world. These publications are listed, with brief details, in *WAY* or *WH*, which you will also find in the library.

Writing magazines often include details about poetry, if not any actual poems. See Further Reading, and other books which list small press magazines, such as the renowned *Light's List*, only £1.50 for hundreds of publications here and abroad.

Shopping around for outlets

Initially you will be spoiled for choice and bewildered, so have a good look round before deciding on the publications which seem to have the most to offer.

It may be simpler to start with a general writing magazine until you have gathered enough information about specific poetry magazines. Or concentrate on those which are published in your area – another way of getting to know other local writers. The Regional Arts Board should be able to provide all the information you need:

- lists of local workshops
- courses
- competitions
- readings and other literary events.

A few mainstream magazines accept poetry and some of them are in the newsagents, for example *This England* and *YES!*, whilst others are on subscription. Although the small press is largely literary, with few magazines having a circulation over 2,000, there are many other publications on subscription, some of them with five-figure circulation figures. They cover every topic under the sun, even poetry sometimes, and occasionally they make payments, usually around £10. For example: *Challenge* (monthly Christian newspaper); *Yorkshire Journal; Desire Direct* ('voluptuous verse and raunchy rhymes').

As there's so much competition to have work accepted, this is where humorous verse comes in useful, although it's not always considered to be real Poetry. Having a wider appeal, however, it stands a better chance of being selected, even publications which

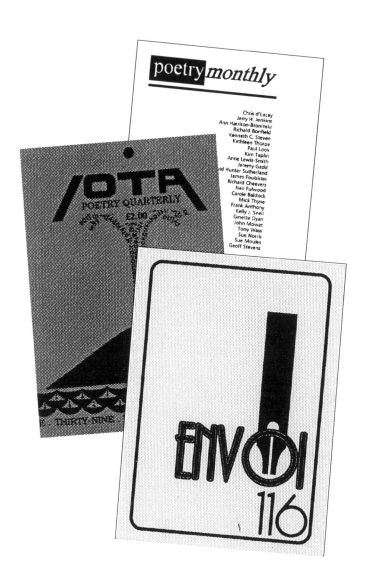

Fig. 13. Small press poetry magazines.

don't take poetry may consider using it as a filler, particularly when topical.

Poems for children
Much children's poetry is funny but it's far from easy to write. Short stories and books for young readers are also difficult, as you will see in the next chapter.

WATCHING OUT FOR THE VANITY PRESS

As a rule, there is very little money to be made out of poetry. Unfortunately, there's a great deal of money to be made from a great many people who write poems, if they fall prey to the vanity press. The fat cats in this trade cream off thousands of pounds from people so desperate to see their work in print that they will fork out £60 for one anthology, when the heftiest hardback blockbuster is rarely more than £20 or, worse still, thousands of pounds to have their own collection printed.

So much has been said about the vanity press that you could write a book about it – but this has still failed to stamp it out. It actually seems to be flourishing: companies persuade punters to part with large sums of money by convincing them that they are the new W H Auden. Sometimes the books are never even printed, while those that are usually end up stacked away in the spare bedroom because no effort was made to market them. It's a hard way to learn about the importance of marketing, but all books need to be properly publicised and distributed so they are available throughout the country.

Judging a book by its cover?
Vanity press is a con trick, and an incredibly successful one because novices and naïve writers often think that if their work is printed, that proves it must be good. A letter in *The Bookseller* pointed out that some people genuinely believe all writers pay to have their work published. If you have any doubts at all about the printers you are dealing with, double-check whether they are vanity press.

QUESTIONS AND ANSWERS

I've seen adverts in loads of magazines and newspapers offering to publish work, so surely they must be genuine?

Caveat emptor: let the buyer beware. Publishers, particularly where poetry is concerned, hardly ever advertise for contributions because they already have so much work on file. Submissions are often invited for work 'which may be difficult to place elsewhere' or using some similarly ambiguous phrase. This could mean little quality control and an overall poor standard of work *but* it can also relate to unusual subjects which are not seen as commercially viable. If you are happy to pay to have your work published, that's one thing. It's quite another when you are persuaded to part with large sums of money, flattered into believing that a company will do everything in their power to ensure that your wonderful words will bring the fame and fortune you so richly deserve.

This company says they will print 1,000 copies of my book and once they've all gone, they'll do another print run and it'll be sold in all the big newsagents. And it'll only cost me £2,000.

When you need a plumber, it's common sense to get two or three estimates, there are now plenty of advertisements for printing books, so ask around. If you contact a local printer about a first collection of poems, you'll find that a plain booklet of about forty pages is generally quite inexpensive. However, acceptance for an anthology is sometimes conditional on your purchasing a copy or it may be offered at a 'specially reduced rate'. And whilst you may be reassured to find that your work is so superior to some of the rest, you could be horrified at the general standard of the contents.

Somebody said I'd end up having to sell all the books myself. That can't be true, surely?

This is where market research comes in handy. Have you ever seen any publications by this company reviewed in magazines, or has there been any mention of the company itself? Are their books in your local bookshop or the library? Have the assistants ever heard of them? Or sold any? Were you impressed by their cover, the layout, the size? The contents? Find out from the company how they plan to market and distribute their publications but remember, it's one thing saying it, quite another doing anything about it.

Last of all, and hardest of all: be painfully honest now. Weren't you just a little taken aback by the extremely enthusiastic response and the fulsome praise of all your work?

ENTERING COMPETITIONS

The Poetry Library produces a selected list each month of around fifteen pages of competitions, although details of prize money are not included. Some prizes can be thousands of pounds whilst others are a percentage of the money received in entry fees. Similarly, entry fees are wide-ranging, particularly as many organisers offer an optional critique – at a price. There are still some free competitions and several which cost under £2.

Some competitions are for charity; others are a one-off. It's becoming more usual to provide an anthology of winning entries, but watch out if the price seems exorbitant. Having paid an entry fee, competitors should surely be entitled to a complimentary copy each, or at a substantial discount. If not, it's worth considering who is going to benefit.

Many organisers start the publicity campaign months ahead, some leave things to the last minute. Most advertise as widely as possible. *Writers News* produces an annual competitions listing and, like all writing magazines, includes details in each issue. *The New Writer* and *Orbis* are known for providing the most comprehensive coverage. There are also sections in *WAY* and *WH*, plus one about the various prizes available. The best thing about winning a prestigious competition, apart from the money, is that publishers will be falling over themselves to snap up your first or next collection.

REVIEWING POETRY

The letters sections in many small press magazines mostly amount to feedback, offering comments on the work published in previous issues. 'Lively correspondence' (*ie* vituperative, acerbic, or just plain bitchy) is always welcome to editors, although they don't all include review sections, usually because some readers don't care for them. Those who do welcome offers from putative reviewers, since they are always inundated with other magazines and books and have to resort to listing those received.

Any payment is usually a token amount, as you get to keep the book. Should it be *Slipshod Sibyls* by Germaine Greer, you've saved yourself £20, but as you're not always given a choice, it could be a bright yellow pamphlet twittering on about somebody's pet mongoose.

Profiting by reviewing

There are several advantages in writing reviews:

- Editors are more likely to accept them than poems.

- You can more easily make a name for yourself.

- It's an excellent way to find out more about poetry and writing in general.

Once your views appear in one magazine, others may want to use your services, providing you temper your criticisms. Keep the word 'constructive' in mind, rather than 'rubbish'. Non-stop sarcasm may be amusing to some readers but many poets are hyper-sensitive. Reviewing is a marvellous opportunity to display your command of the English language; use it so that people look forward to finding out what you have to say, not to see who you're having a go at this time.

Starting to write reviews

Learning how to write reviews of poetry is not that hard. Try following this outline:

1. Brief introduction about the poet's background and the theme of the collection.

2. Certain poems singled out for praise and/or criticism.

3. Analysis of structure, form and style, illustrated by quotes.

4. Summing up.

HAVING A GO AT PERFORMANCE POETRY

There is no denying that some poems should be read out loud and others read in books, although some poets do not do justice to their work when performing. But you can learn about the basics:

- delivery
- stage presence
- timing
- selecting pieces appropriate for a particular venue.

Not everyone is prepared to put in that kind of effort and, on occasion, tumultuous applause at readings is more the result of relief than appreciation.

The current popularity of poetry is a chicken and egg situation: is it because of the spread of performance poetry (itself in the wake of stand-up comedy) or are the greater opportunities for performance the result of the increasing interest in poetry? National Poetry Day in October has guaranteed that throughout the country many cities, towns and even villages will arrange something to celebrate the occasion. Keep an eye on the local paper, listings magazines and the library for information about poetry events, or contact the Regional Arts Board.

Making your debut

Performing can be extremely nerve-racking, so you may prefer to sit quietly, inwardly digesting, on your first visit. It's more reassuring to find out what's involved: the kind of people who turn up and the sort of poetry which goes down well. If you have any questions, ask away, since the people there will be happy to help you out; the MC or whoever's in charge can arrange for one of the other poets to take you under his or her wing. Once familiar with the venue and the people, that in itself gives you more confidence, if not to strut your stuff, at least to face the limelight for a few minutes. Such events are invariably very relaxed, good-humoured and welcoming to all newcomers.

There are a few points of etiquette which you should observe:

- Never talk during somebody else's performance.

- If you arrive when somebody is performing, don't try to sneak into the room, no matter now quietly, until they have finished.

- Try to avoid ordering drinks or leaving during a performance.

- Support any events organised by the group. Guest evenings are an opportunity to see some famous poets in action.

Above all, if the average time per reading is five minutes, or the organiser insists that there's only time for each performer to do two or three poems, do not work your way through your entire *oeuvre*.

And finally, when it is your turn, you may be convinced that it's the worst thing since sitting your driving test, but it can turn out to be one of the most enjoyable.

the Dead Good Poets Society

NEW POETS! OLD POETS!

Come along - share your work!

Admission free. Good beer. Friendly audience.
New readers get priority (Get your name down with the MC)
5 minutes per poet - max 18 on the night.
(Please perform your own work)

Open Floor Night

1st Wed of the month, 3rd Room
Everyman Bistro, Hope St, Liverpool 1
Starts at 8.00 pm.

*Watch out for our seasonal programme of guests: top
national, local and international poets. We also
run exchanges and workshops.
For information, or if you want to get involved, call:*

David on 767 9802

supported
by
north west arts

Supported
by
L.C.C.

Fig. 14. Flyer for performance poetry.

> **To have an audience sit in pin-drop silence and win their applause is an amazing experience.**

CASE STUDIES

Dexter stages a protest

Dexter reads about what seems a genuine invitation to contribute to a local small press anthology. The title is vague, giving little idea of the theme, so he submits four very different poems but the editor rings up to say he's sure Dexter 'could do better if he tried'. When he points out that his work has been widely published, the editor replies that 'he doesn't doubt it', in a tone conveying the exact opposite. Helpfully, he sends Dexter a selection of his own work, which 'has been compared to John Donne'. It would have the famous poet digging his way out of the grave, never mind turning in it.

Brent is upstaged

Brent is invited to a festival run by an old friend. One of the star attractions is a successful poet known for refusing interviews, but there's the possibility of an informal chat, so Brent arranges a commission from a renowned literary magazine. At the reading the MC announces that there are two local poets as support; all three will do two twenty-minute readings. Celebrity Guest is not pleased. Barely ten minutes into his performance the MC advances upon the stage, clapping loudly, announcing a fifteen-minute interval. Later, asked why he cut Celebrity Guest short, he retorts: 'Well, it felt like twenty minutes.' Even Brent realises that there is little chance of a chat, interview, or a civil 'goodnight'.

Katrina gets stuck in the early stages

Katrina makes a couple of suggestions to a leading newspaper. Although they are turned down, the letter is friendly and assures her that her details are on file. She then comes up with something sure-fire: a leading company hires a woman poet to improve customer relations by adding a uniquely personal touch to correspondence. When an unexpected lull enables her to catch up with her reading, including the paper's Sunday supplement from last month, Katrina discovers the leading article features said poet. She must look thoroughly unprofessional but consoles herself that 'great minds think alike'. At least she is on the right track, even if her bright idea has already been used by somebody else.

DISCUSSION POINTS

1. Why do you want to write poetry? Is it for publication or performance?

2. Do you prefer to work alone? How would you get in contact with other poets?

3. Can you develop your interest in other areas, such as working in schools, running an appraisal service, organising events?

ASSIGNMENT

Choose a couple of books about writing poetry, to assess which gives the best advice for the kind of writing you want to do. Then compare a recently published collection of poetry with something you studied in school, such as Wordsworth or Wilfred Owen.

6
Writing Fiction for Publication

If prose is your forté, there are several things to be considered:

- how to write short stories
- where to have them published
- the market for young readers
- novel-writing and the different genres.

STARTING OFF WITH SHORT STORIES

A quick look at *WAY* will reveal sections on novels, non-fiction and poetry. Short stories? Half a page on outlets, plus half a column of competitions and the same for publishers. Many people regard the short story as a practice run for the novel rather than an art form in itself. Yet, if poetry is considered the finest of writing, surely the best short stories come a close second? Indeed, it seems that writers *are* increasingly more interested in short stories than poems.

As with poetry, the great disadvantage is that there are far more people who write stories than read them, hence the demise of so many outlets, from literary greats like *Panurge* and *IRON*, to the short-lived *Pulp Fiction* and *Saffron Editions*, for those who prefer more popular literature.

Another disheartening fact is that many excellent stories published in the small press are not, in general, considered sufficiently mainstream (*ie* commercial) to interest the big publishing houses.

There are many first class exponents of the short story, and to have any chance at all of joining that number:

- read all you can
- study books on the subject
- make a habit of reading reviews.

Reviews are invaluable for sorting the wheat from the chaff, whilst

Fig. 15. Small press prose magazines.

allowing for the fact that everybody has different tastes. There is, alas, something as irresistible about books which are scornfully castigated as those which are praised to the skies.

Learning the nuts and bolts of writing

Adopting a professional approach to writing can be helped by going on a course or attending workshops. Even if you end up disillusioned with your own efforts, you will learn enough to know how to apply your particular talents to another form of writing. It also helps you to decide exactly what kind of audience you are aiming for. People read for lots of reasons, primarily for enjoyment which for the majority means some form of escapism.

Nonetheless, the best of what's called 'five-minute fiction', frequently women's magazine stories, is as difficult to write as serious literature. Obviously, it appeals to a specific market, one paying very well indeed, which is why so many writers aspire to it.

CHOOSING YOUR MARKETS

Many newsstand magazines firmly state that they will not accept unsolicited manuscripts. They mean what they say, so don't waste their time, and yours, sending them any packages. It doesn't mean you cannot enquire as to the possibility of publication – especially when the editor of one monthly glossy returns your work suggesting you approach another editor. Publishers like D C Thomson, who produce a number of magazine titles, are well known for being sympathetic towards writers, and making prompt payments. Appraisal services and agencies, such as Midland Exposure (see Useful Addresses), provide helpful advice about possible outlets.

Knowing your niche

Short stories are often summarily divided into two main categories:

- the literary
- the popular.

Never the twain shall meet, according to the fans of each. Literary is considered pretentious or obscure whilst popular fiction is held to be contributing to the dumbing down of literature. So, banquet or beefburger? What's important is that it's cooked properly and tastes good; the best examples of each kind are equally well crafted. Many readers, after all, are quite happy to dip into either, as the mood takes them, and the same thing applies to some writers as well. One prolific writer based most of her stories on letters in the problem pages of magazines, offerings which succeeded because they were genuine human interest.

As many short stories are published which you personally won't think much of, as there is fiction so brilliant you feel you may give up writing there and then.

> **It's reading, and lots and lots of it, which is the only way to discover exactly the right outlet for your work.**

Not only is reading enjoyable, but you are learning all the time, particularly as all the contents of your chosen outlets need to be studied in order to make sure your submissions are along the same lines. For example, a precise definition of the difference between pornographic and erotic is always tricky; when submitting stories to women's magazines you need to be very sure about what's considered erotic and what's romantic. Interestingly, whatever your opinion of publications like *Penthouse* and *Playboy*, such magazines have an excellent reputation for serious fiction, with submissions from many famous authors.

Readings

This is the term used for short stories broadcast on radio. The Radio 4 slot for short stories is probably the best known: contact the Editor, Readings, at the BBC. For local BBC stations it's the Assistant Editor, such as for *Write Now* on Radio Merseyside. Some independent stations may also consider short stories. For general interest, programmes such as Radio 4's *Kaleidoscope* are well known for arts coverage and *Classic FM* often features interviews with authors and book reviews.

Payment for readings may be minimal but your work is reaching a wide audience. Since writing for the listener is very different to writing work that is to be read, study it first before submitting anything. There is a useful handbook available, *Writing for the BBC* (see Further Reading), or you could contact an independent radio producer (see *WAY*), though they tend to specialise in drama rather than fiction.

Submitting short stories to small press magazines

The small or independent press has a range of publications, catering for every kind of taste. There are also many magazines which are useful sources of information. (See Further Reading.) Some of them actually make payments, though not enough to retire on. Oddly enough there are now a large number of short story competitions, almost as if to compensate for the fact that there are fewer outlets.

Many of these offer magazine publication or an anthology for the winning entries. Some magazines, like *Story Cellar* or *Figments*, run regular competitions for subscribers. There are also small presses, for example, Piper's Ash, whose quarterly competitions invite entries for publication in a chapbook or collection of stories or poetry, for which royalties are paid.

Approaching an agent

Once a few of your stories have appeared in prestigious publications, enough to form an impressive debut collection, you could consider approaching an agent or a publisher. However, getting a collection

Competition News ...

If you are writing to anyone here for further information always include SAE. Unless otherwise stated, all competition entries should be in English, unpublished and not currently entered for any other competition, typed, double-spaced on one side only of white A4 paper, with wide margins. Poems can be single spaced on separate sheets. All pages should be clearly numbered. No identifying marks normally appear on MS. which should include a separate title page giving name, address and telephone number. Where official entry forms or special requirements are part of the rules of entry, this will be stated. If an envelope marked 'results' is enclosed, most competition organisers will now supply them on request.

Kent Literature Festival is inviting entries for a short story competition for £1,350. Judges Alison Chisholm and Iain Pattison. Fee: £3.50 per entry. and entry form send SAE to 3 Carver Road, Herne Hill, London SE24 9LS.

Bi-annual Haiku Competition, £300 in prize money. Each competition

CRABBE MEMORIAL POETRY COMPETITION   31 May
Prizes: £150, £100, £75
Adjudicators: Jo Shapcott & Harry Chambers
Fee? Length: 40 lines
Open to anyone with Suffolk links
Contact: John Watts, Kingfisher Barn, Kings Lane,
Weston, Beccles, Suffolk NR34 8TR

JACKSON'S ARM POETRY PAMPHLET COMPETITION   31 May
Fee: £14; for a collection of 16 pages (page = 30 lines, excluding titles)
either 1 long poem or a number of poems

Diary of Events   49

The Writers News Diary of Events

Should you wish to have an entry included please complete the coupon on page F

Date	Event	Venue	Cost	Contact	Phone
		RESIDENTIAL COURSES			
17-19 Jan	New dream journeys – a writing course	Missenden Abbey, Bucks	POA	Missenden Abbey	01494 890296
31 Jan-2 Feb	Contemporary British poetry	Missenden Abbey, Bucks	POA	Missenden Abbey	01494 890296

Fig. 16. Useful information from writers' magazines
(Taken from *Freelance Market News*, *The New Writer* and *Writers News*).

of short stories published seems to be more difficult than it is with poetry and selling it is just as much hard work.

WRITING FOR CHILDREN AND TEENAGERS

Some of today's best novels are aimed at teenagers. This may seem a market worth considering, especially as these books, although shorter, appear little different from those for adults, frequently and increasingly dealing with similar themes.

Looking at teenagers' books

Ironically, labelling books 'for teenagers' is probably the kiss of death where that age group is concerned. Non-readers never look twice at them, whilst avid readers bypass any intermediate stage, going straight on to cult or classic novels. For the budding bookworm, teenage angst reaches its high point with the awful realisation that they will never have the time to read every one of their favourite type of books. It is usually down to parents, teachers and librarians to introduce them to books written specifically for teenagers, which results in enough of a market to ensure that publishers continue to produce them.

Looking at children's books

As far as younger age groups are concerned, writing for children is harder than most people think.

> **Just because something appears to be short and simple does not mean it is easy to do.**

Far from it, if you consider the limit both to vocabulary and to themes. Another constraint these days is that it is subjected to the politically correct. Enid Blyton fans had best stick to re-reading her books rather than attempt to emulate her work.

There are many anecdotes about writers whose books came about because they made up their own bedtime stories. Considering how fiendishly critical one's children can be, in this instance they make an indulgent audience, usually because said tales revolve around them. But that's no guarantee that they will appeal to other children.

Using illustrations

Another big mistake is to confuse having a knack for turning out pictures with the ability to provide illustrations of the kind publishers require. This also applies to collaborations; you may admire your best friend's arty streak, but if the publishing house is not impressed they won't be inclined to leniency no matter how brilliant your tales. They much prefer to use the services of their own team of illustrators. It works in reverse, of course; the most gifted illustrator will be let down by shoddily written stories.

Carrying out market research

Follow the usual rules:

- take a good look at what's on the shelves
- read *Bookseller* magazine
- ask your local bookstore or library if you can borrow back copies of their publishers' catalogues.

One advantage of writing children's books is that they seem to have a far longer shelf life than books for adults. Hardbacks usually reappear a year later in paperback format, but are generally remaindered after a short time. An increasing number of books now get only one bite of the cherry since they are published as 'originals', *ie* paperbacks.

Finding work as a regular contributor
As children are notorious collectors, series are extremely popular with publishers and they are not necessarily written by the same person. Sometimes entire teams of writers contribute to the work of a pseudonymous author. You may not like the idea of such formula writing, but it does mean your foot is firmly in the doorway. Besides, if you are an expert on subjects as diverse as horses, computers or the supernatural, why not put your knowledge to good use?

The same kind of material comes in for non-fiction books. There are always complaints about falling standards of literacy, but children who have difficulty learning to read because they are not interested in stories will get the hang of it a lot sooner if they are fascinated by subjects such as dinosaurs or outer space and want to find out more about it.

WRITING NOVELS

Ask any bestselling author for one piece of advice and invariably it will be this: read, read, read.

> **That's what being a writer boils down to: read lots, think plenty, and only then start writing.**

This doesn't mean to say that you are then guaranteed publication; getting a novel published is often likened to winning the lottery, the odds against it are so high.

Few writers are deterred, knowing that famous authors like Frederick Forsyth were rejected time and time again. There's even a book on the subject (*Unpublishable!* by Elaine Borish). Similarly, there are many Cinderella stories of first-time authors being snapped up for large sums of money, Michael Ridpath being the classic case. On the other hand, the week after the 1997 Booker shortlist was announced, only 2,000 copies were sold – of all six titles.

They do say that if a book is good it is bound to be published, although one publisher reckoned that in twenty years only two decent manuscripts from the **slush pile** turned up. Yet in the long run it matters little, for whether the intention is to see your book in print, or to have a book published and become rich and famous, anyone who has an urge to write a book will go right ahead and do it. The more serious they are about it, the more likely they are to complete it. To borrow the *Mastermind* phrase: 'I've started, so I'll finish' marks an attitude which separates novelist from novice.

Watching out for the pitfalls

In her book *From an Editor's Desk*, Suzanne Ruthven, editor of *The New Writer*, reckons that on average you can expect to write your novel seven times. That's her argument for switching from typewriter to computer, but it gives you an idea of the task ahead.

Keeping copies

A word-processed book can also be saved to disk (twice, if you're edgy), whereas carbon copies are a real bind. *Always* keep a copy. It's one thing to have hysterics at the antics of Blackadder after accidentally burning Dr Johnson's dictionary, but you're more likely to end up having a nervous breakdown if you ever lost your one and only manuscript. Nigel Watts, who won the Betty Trask prize for his first novel *The Life Game*, lost his fourth book when he was mugged in New York. And what do you bet he wishes he had £1 for every time somebody said: 'Hey, what a great idea for a novel'?

DECIDING WHAT KIND OF NOVEL TO WRITE

In the adult market, alongside the modern novel, there are many different genres:

- crime
- erotica
- fantasy
- historical
- horror
- humour
- romance
- thrillers.

For paperbacks the greatest number of sales come under the very unhelpful heading of 'general', but this is followed by mystery and science fiction. However, for hardbacks, sales of general and mystery are very similar with science fiction again in third place.

As with themes, settings and characters, genre itself tends to go in cycles. The '60s saw a huge boom in historical novels and many people are now forecasting a resurgence, following the tremendous popularity of characters like Ellis Peters' Cadfael, and Falco, Lindsey Davis' Roman detective. Formerly, historicals frequently divided their time between gripping romance and some kind of mystery, but the latter now takes precedence with the emergence of the overly inquisitive hero or heroine.

Similarly, fantasy is currently enjoying a huge success; approaching the Millennium really does seem to have opened the floodgates. It's a genre said to flourish in times of depression or repression, the so-called Golden Age being during the '30s. As for horror, that seems to have come to a crossroads, either descending to ever more gore-splattered epics, or aspiring to something far more sophisticated, so subtle in fact that in the hands of the best writers it is more nightmarish than ever.

There is also the cross-genre, increasingly coming into its own, such as historical detective novels. Occasionally this doesn't fit any known pigeon-hole, being a real mixed bag: erotic historical horror, or historical horror erotica? The latest classification is 'contemporary urban fiction', christened 'New Brit' by *The Guardian*. According to Penguin there is an increasing 20-something market. Publishers prefer it if you stick to one easily labelled type of book because it's far easier for them to market. So much so that any success in a particular field, like crime, means you have little chance of finding out whether the grass really is greener (or the roses sweeter), writing a romantic novel.

Taking the first steps in novel writing

Even if you are bursting to get started on your book – wait. There is no harm in making notes, indeed it is often recommended, since there are many different ways of writing a novel. Some authors meticulously plan the whole thing in advance with wall charts, calendars, maps and CVs for all the main characters. Others have a rough idea of what they want to say, sit themselves down and let it all flow (or not, as the case may be); for them, the hard work comes at the editing stage. First and foremost, however, learn the ground rules and make it easier on yourself: read a few books on the subject. Writing a novel is one of the hardest of tasks, which may be why it is universally admired. Whether you trust in organisation or inspiration, it needs researching. After that, it's a question of stamina, keeping your head down for the next few hundred pages.

CASE STUDIES

Dexter sits in judgement

Dexter has a go at short stories now and again though he rarely bothers submitting them. This one, originally a poem, has turned out well and he sends it to a magazine which sometimes takes his non-fiction work. The editor is full of enthusiasm but the manuscript comes back, heavily edited, accompanied by a request 'to make a few changes'. Well, £20 is £20, and although Shelley-Danielle says he should ring up and tell the editor exactly what he can do with his magazine, Dexter sets to work. He discovers that the editor himself has made a few errors; not everybody these days understands the correct usage of the gerund. Dexter feels obliged to point out the need for amendments but there's no reply to his letter, nor the two reminders. Somehow, he doesn't have the heart to ring up.

Brent discovers that he should judge not, lest he be judged

Brent is asked to adjudicate a short story competition for a small press magazine. It's time-consuming, not very well paid and rather boring, but he's also been asked to provide a report. At least it's one way of getting his name known. Unfortunately, once he's ploughed through all the manuscripts and comes to write the report, he is not in the best of moods. The three winning entries receive grudging approval but he can't be bothered to provide constructive criticism and is scathing about the rest. Surprisingly, the editor doesn't mind – a bit of controversy means lively correspondence and better sales. Some months later Brent comes across a story in another magazine, written by one of the entrants, in which one repulsively villainous character has a name remarkably similar to his.

Katrina misjudges her timing

As books editor, Katrina is sure she has come up with a cast-iron idea for a bestseller. She also thinks it would be foolish to waste time and effort if she cannot be sure of publication. After mulling it over for several months, she rings round and eventually finds a publisher who is cautiously optimistic and agrees to consider it. She visits her friendly neighbourhood bookstore to look at the novels covering the same ground. There are quite a few more than when she did her initial market research, perusing publishers' catalogues. Nearly a year later, when the publisher finally replies, a lot more titles have appeared. Her proposal is turned down – 'it has now been done to death'.

DISCUSSION POINTS

1.   Are you a marathon runner, or a sprinter? You may be able to combine writing both short stories and novels but each requires different disciplines.

2.   What kind of stories/books do you tend to read? What kind are you planning to write and do you have a particular age group in mind?

3.   Are you prepared to put in a lot of work on a subject which interests you, such as research for a historical novel?

ASSIGNMENT

Choose your favourite short story and/or novel. Write down all the reasons why you like it, as well as anything which you feel could be improved.

7

Writing Non-Fiction
for Publication

This chapter sets out to show how valuable non-fiction can be for all writers:

- why writing non-fiction is good for your career and how to make a start
- investigating the wide range of markets
- experimenting with the different types of non-fiction.

AIMING HIGH

Even if your sole ambition has always been to write a novel you may not be able to give up the day job, but it can still be connected with writing:

- running workshops or courses
- working in schools
- operating an appraisal service
- working on a magazine
- working for a publisher.

Writing non-fiction can help your career

The great advantage of non-fiction is that it enhances the odds of producing a publishable book, by improving the necessary skills:

- writing ability
- research
- organisation
- discipline
- networking.

There are some disadvantages. You may be unable to:

- find the time
- find the motivation
- manage without the money.

A complex juggling act must be mastered to succeed as a novelist; even the huge sacrifice of giving up a steady job may have to be considered. More optimistically, things often tend to evolve for writers. Step by step you graduate from fillers to features, from books of non-fiction to fiction itself. Many novels are written by journalists and other non-fiction writers.

BEGINNING TO WRITE NON-FICTION

There is little opportunity to start learning about non-fiction from courses, other than journalism. Fortunately, many publications have guidelines available, one of the most useful for advice on contributing articles being the booklet *Writing for Reader's Digest* (see Further Reading).

> The process of writing non-fiction is every bit as creative as writing poetry and prose.

Without ideas and inspiration, nobody can write anything. It's the most creative ideas which make non-fiction successful, whether a completely original idea or a clever twist of a hackneyed theme. Many magazine editors happily welcome a different angle on Easter, Halloween or Christmas. However, most people go on writing courses to learn about having their poetry, short stories and novels published. When urged to aim for non-fiction markets they consider they are being fobbed off, but there is *always* a market for non-fiction, with a choice of different writing forms:

- fillers
- news items
- reviews
- articles
- features
- interviews.

Any or all of these can lead to your becoming a regular

contributor (and to a steady income), perhaps writing your own column or series.

FINDING SUITABLE MARKETS

If your aim is literary, the smallest of small press magazines normally includes some information about other publications. The main purpose of some writing magazines is providing marketing information about both newsstand and small press publications.

For information about publishers, the weekly publication *Bookseller* is the best place to look, whilst *The Guardian* on Monday and Saturday includes an ample media advertising section. But dream jobs invariably mean a London address. Mandi Norwood, editor of *Cosmopolitan*, was so determined to succeed that she accepted she had to move down south. Those of us north of Watford have to allow for the fact that every advert receives a colossal response, with any reaction being the usual 'don't call us...'. Of course, once you've decided to have a clear out and 'filed' your papers in the waste-paper bin, that's when somebody rings with an offer you can't refuse.

STARTING SMALL

Writing fillers
A **filler** is a short item, several of which are used in every issue of nearly every magazine. One of the most renowned markets for fillers of all kinds is *The Reader's Digest*. They may not come in all different sizes, but they certainly appear in all different shapes:

- letters
- trivia/factual items
- humorous items
- puzzles.

Most writing magazines devote a page to the various markets and there are several books on the subject.

The pros
Fillers have several advantages:

- usually well paid
- constant demand

- those not topical can come in useful any time
- wide variety
- quick and easy.

That is to say, they *look* quick and easy, but that's the expert touch although advertising invariably emphasises that these are a guaranteed money spinner. Like all writing, there is an art to producing them and it's an extremely useful skill to be able to write something succinctly, particularly for editing. Generally speaking, fillers are ideal for those for whom writing is likely to be their favourite hobby, combining a good chance of publication with the occasional remuneration.

The cons
Some writers feel that there are disadvantages in concentrating on the filler market:

- time-consuming
- the effort involved far outweighs the rewards
- amateurish
- ephemeral.

One problem when submitting letters is that they are not universally acknowledged. Some newspapers do advise if they are not going to be published, whilst magazines confirm when work is held on file. Unless you're a regular reader of a publication, it's difficult to tell whether anything has been used until the cheque arrives. If you want to try another outlet with the same piece, you should wait at least six months.

Sadly, the most brilliant piece of work in the most prestigious publication is soon past its sell by date. The career-minded tend to regard writing fillers as a starting point, although it needs professional ability to succeed. Nonetheless, if you have a flair for letter writing or a knack for cracking jokes, you could specialise in this area to help boost your income. More importantly, it's another way to make a name for yourself.

Writing greetings cards

If this strikes you as a promising market, send a large SAE to The Greeting Card Association (see Useful Addresses) for a list of members. Market research could not be simpler: study the cards in newsagents; most companies have their address on the back and some invite submissions of material. They are also happy to supply you with guidelines and sample cards, *but* it can be a difficult market to break into and your work may be rejected on the grounds that they've already received something similar. Great minds think alike? Even allowing for coincidence, you can see for yourself that many cards are based on very elderly jokes; a few companies delicately hint that they don't object to 'recycled' work. But there's really no guarantee that your material won't be used – without your being any the wiser.

If you are interested in this market, perhaps a better route to success is to team up with somebody artistic, plus your friendly neighbourhood printer, and produce your own cards. It may prove a wise investment because if they become popular you can branch out into postcards, posters, badges, booklets – including poetry collections.

Writing news items

Although more serious in intent and style, many of the advantages and disadvantages of fillers apply to news items. Nonetheless, there are several reasons why they are considered to be a few steps above fillers. News items:

- give a writer authority
- gain entreé to two outlets
- are valuable for networking.

It's always useful for a writer to be considered an expert on a particular subject, although writing news items sometimes amounts to rephrasing press releases. To ensure your suggestions for news items are acceptable, you need access to mailing lists (primary source), not something you've spotted in a magazine (secondary source).

Benefits to you and to the editor
Even when press releases also go directly to the same outlet, your offer to provide a news item gives the editor a second chance to take note of it, saving staff in-house the bother of writing it up. The organisation issuing the press release will appreciate your promotional efforts which can even mean more work if they reckon you've made a better job of publicity than the original press release. Writing press releases is another art form worth reading up on, ready for the day you have something of your own to promote, such as a book.

Action stations at the Gateway

Chester Gateway's new artistic director. Deborah Shaw, has already been involved with the theatre. Her imaginative adaptation of The Thirty-Nine Steps was staged there in June. She is looking forward to continuing the theatre's success and its commitment to new work, world premières and a varied programme.

As a result of its recent Lottery award of £290,000 the theatre will be refurbishing the bar, the cafè bar and front-of-house area and upgrading sound, lighting, heating and ventilation. The Manweb Studio Theatre should be completed by January 1998, making an ideal space for comedy, fringe performances, dance, music, amateur shows and workshops, and the youth theatre base.

The theatre plans to make another bid later in the year, to the Arts for Everyone programme, to raise funds for new commissions, outreach work, education and initiatives involving young people. Meanwhile, a series of fortnightly creative writing classes, aimed at 15-year-olds and upwards, starts 16 September. Contact Adam Fresco, youth theatre director, for details.

Finally, anyone curious about what goes on backstage can find out more on The Open Day, Saturday, 6 September. For more information, contact Jo Beggs, Chester Gateway Theatre Trust Ltd. Hamilton Place, Chester CH1 2BH. Tel: 01244 344238.

Carole Baldock

Fig. 17. Sample news-writing item (*Theatre*).

It can be extremely useful getting into an editor's good books by promoting their magazine, but never take it for granted that this guarantees having all your suggestions immediately accepted for publication. The rules governing suitability and space always apply. Nevertheless, good, reliable work will impress the editor in whose publication the news item appears. Now you have:

- kept two people happy
- enhanced your future chances of publication
- updated your CV
- and added some useful sample writing to your portfolio.

The last could prove the deciding factor when approaching yet another editor, and there is also the possibility of other editors contacting you after reading your work.

Writing reviews

Reviewing is frequently overlooked, surprisingly, considering its potential – you always receive some form of recompense, even if it's payment in kind. Yet it barely rates a mention in writing manuals and there appears to be only one book on the subject. Reviewing has similar advantages to news items and is valuable for acquiring skills:

- editing
- analysis
- research.

Frequently dealt with in-house, there are still plenty of outlets. A good way to start your writing career is by offering your services to the local paper or listings magazine. One theatre editor complains of having to go out every night of the week, with no say in the choice of productions. There are also other areas in which you can specialise:

- art
- film
- music
- leisure activities (restaurants, tourist attractions)
- books.

Reviews are useful to a non-fiction writer as a stepping stone to bigger and better things: articles, features and interviews. Building up a good relationship with theatres, publishers and so on means you are often in at the start of something promising. Publishers sometimes help you out with research, while theatres may suggest interviews with the star of the next production, something you should have no difficulty in selling since interviews are perennially popular with magazines.

Setting the tone

There is also more scope when composing reviews. They can be as brief as fillers, in which case your summarising needs to be equally succinct, or as long as 500 words, allowing you to express an opinion. The tone can be humorous, which is often preferred for fillers, or as straightforward as a news item, depending on the particular publication. Like most news items, reviews have an introduction and draw a conclusion, but the body of the text is virtually yours to do with as you will, providing each point you make is backed up with examples.

INCREASING YOUR OPPORTUNITIES

Tackling articles and features

The terms 'article' and 'feature' tend to be interchangeable, but here article refers to a generalised piece of writing, feature being more specific. For example, an article might deal with the detrimental effects single parent families have on society, whilst a feature concentrates on one family and how the mother copes with three children at university. Although there is an increasing demand for the 'mini-article', at around 300–500 words similar to a review, the average length for articles is 800–2,500 words. As you know by now, length means what the editor says it means, *not* a couple of hundred words either way.

> **Market research is essential, since the contents and aims of all magazines and newspapers vary.**

A national survey in which 64 per cent say 'yes' might appear in *The Daily Mail* as 'an overwhelming success', whilst *The Guardian* says 'opinion is evenly divided'. All publications have their own house-style, ranging from particular rules of grammar to the number of words per sentence. Are you prepared to amend your usual writing style to fit in? And do you address your work to the features editor or the arts editor, or is it more appropriate for the women's page? The simple answer is to highlight the most suitable angle: educational, technological, family.

Illustrations

If you are handy with a camera, the chances of acceptance are even higher if you offer illustrations. Otherwise, when possible suggest where illustrations can be obtained; press offices provide photographs for interviews to do with the entertainment industry.

Seasonal ideas

Seasonal or topical suggestions are made well in advance, and the calendar itself provides inspiration. Much material stands a better chance of serious consideration in August's traditional 'silly season', when little else is going on.

Lead times

One advantage of being a regular contributor is that you get into the habit of starting your next batch once the last lot of work has been published. However, when first approaching any editor, always remember **lead times**:

- weekly: two months in advance
- monthly: four to six months
- quarterly: six to eight months.

If in doubt – ring.

Topical events

Conversely, you sometimes stand a better chance of having some hot topic squeezed into a daily paper. It's a lot of hard work, dropping everything at a moment's notice, and puts you under a great deal of pressure, so make sure it's worth doing. Infuriating to find you've missed the boat, but many topical events come in at a later date using a different angle.

Updating

Magazines are said to run in four-year cycles, so you could dust off your best articles, rewriting them for another market. Obviously your work will be brand new, but if you keep cuttings on issues you have already written about, they can be updated, particularly if they first appeared in a publication which subsequently folded.

Writing interviews

> **Interviews are probably the key to success in non-fiction.**

Press offices are eager to have their clients interviewed, supplying press packs and photographs and setting up interviews. These can be carried out in a variety of ways:

- face-to-face
- over the phone
- via correspondence, by sending a questionnaire.

With the first two, you can either take notes or record the interview; taping means no argument about what was actually said.

Most interviewees appreciate being sent a questionnaire in advance, giving them time to marshall their thoughts. Even with meticulous preparation not all interviews are smooth sailing, sometimes taking ages to set up. Film stars are the trickiest to get hold of, yet stars of the music and publishing world are usually at your disposal.

The big advantage of interviews is that even newsstand glossies will take a chance on an unknown writer who comes up with a good idea or an interesting angle. Most people think the main purpose is for celebrities to plug their latest books, films, plays or whatever; nobody, no matter how famous they are, turns down free publicity. This means interviews galore in the daily papers, the Sunday papers, listings magazine, monthly magazines and so on.

Tailoring interviews

The important thing to remember, along with each publication's *raison d'être*, is that each interview has a particular focus. The readership of one magazine might expect to learn about the star's childhood, another their views on health and fitness, a third their latest relationship. The interviewer must prepare questions relating to the subject matter required. Similarly, the style of the piece should be dictated by that of the magazine. Interviewees who wish to be taken seriously get rather annoyed if their words of wisdom end up in a section taking the mickey, such as *Q's* notorious 'Who does X think he is?'

Alongside the 'big exclusive', the highly illustrated double-page spread, many non-fiction writers rely on interviews as research for more everyday articles. Even the most mundane subject, especially one that is topical, gains something with a few wise words from an expert, in other words an interview in miniature. Articles also sometimes take the form of a survey, which means interviewing several different people in order to provide a rounded view.

Watching for possible problems

Interviewing is not just a pleasant chat:

- Make sure the interviewee keeps to the point.
- Anticipate the best way to interrupt, politely of course, if time runs out and you want to move on to another area.
- Encourage the interviewee to discuss a tricky area.
- Plan what to do if you dry up or run out of questions.

No matter how well-prepared, it can be difficult when you come

INTERVIEW QUESTIONNAIRE: PLAYWRIGHT TIM FIRTH
(Preston Front)

- Do you do other writing besides plays? What's your next favourite?

- If you weren't a writer, what other career would you have followed?

- Which is harder for a new writer: to have a play staged or to have a TV series accepted?

- What would you say was your biggest break?

- What ambitions would you most like to see fulfilled?

- What three basic steps would you recommend to help new writers, for example: methods of working, selling your work, coming up with the goods as required?

- Does writing come easily to you? Do you ever get blocked and if so, how do you overcome it?

- How do you organise your time when writing?

- Which is your own particular favourite piece of work?

- Who are your favourite playwrights? What one play do you wish you had written?

- Who would you say has had a lot of influence on your writing, in the fields of literature, music, the arts?

- Are any of your characters based on real people, or are there local people convinced that they must have inspired you?

- What was your worst/most embarrassing rejection?

- The most satisfying/unexpected success?

- One piece of advice you would give your children?

Fig. 18. Sample interview questionnaire.

to the last in a series of interviews. It's easy to get fed up asking the same questions over and over again – but the finished article shouldn't give the reader that impression. Similarly, when transcribing your notes, whether written (a certain cure for scribbling, since you must decipher what the interviewee actually said) or taped, you will curse the garrulous.

CASE STUDIES

Dexter finds the writing business can be unpredictable

Dexter's first published pieces appeared courtesy of an editor who has just taken over a brand new Sunday supplement. Dexter is delighted to continue their working relationship by providing the occasional review of classical music. Everything goes very well at first and there are hints of his own column in the near future. However, the advertising is not all it should be, but rather than improve that area the publishers decide to economise by moving the editor sideways to join the staff on another publication. Somebody else will take on this job as well as his own. As Dexter knows, new brooms sweep clean, usually brushing all existing arrangements aside.

Brent finds that oversights are just not funny

Brent, rather than forking out a subscription to magazines and requesting contributors' guidelines, occasionally writes asking for a back issue review copy for research purposes. The most useful information is earmarked, whether for potential interviews or news items. Impressed to discover in a three month old copy of a writing magazine that somebody has calculated that payment for fillers in one publication works out at £100 per 1,000 words, he writes to the editor, suggesting an in-depth article. The reply is prompt, courteous and points out that the last issue carried a half-page feature about the same subject.

Katrina gets involved in some funny business

Katrina always studies the media section of the national press and sends off her CV and cuttings where applicable. Sometimes there's a response – the usual letter of thanks advising that her details have gone on file. This time, having written to a PO box in Nottingham, the reply is by return and via the telephone. The editor of a new comedy magazine is extremely keen to use more female contributors. Katrina is asked to supply some feature ideas and any fillers she happens to have, and the dummy copy will be sent to her shortly. The trouble is, comedy publications are notorious for having an extremely short shelf life, but at least it's being published in London.

DISCUSSION POINTS

1. Which sources do you think will provide the most useful information for your needs?

2. Which of the different kinds of non-fiction do you most enjoy reading?

3. Do you have material which could be adapted for a particular market?

ASSIGNMENT

Even if you are quite determined that nothing is going to stop you from writing your novel (one day), see what you can make of one short form of non-fiction and one long.

8
Making the Most of Opportunities

Even if writing is a hobby rather than a career, all writers have ambitions and there are various ways of achieving them through networking:

- deciding on your priorities
- seeking suitable outlets
- getting to know more editors, doing more work for each
- expanding your networks
- considering all the possibilities of writing-related work.

SETTING PERSONAL GOALS

Making assessments from time to time is useful for deciding what you hope to achieve. Writers have all kinds of different goals:

- Publication in a particular magazine, or for a specific market.
- Winning competitions, or having work chosen for an anthology or a collection.
- Branching out into a related field.
- Experimenting with a totally new form of writing.
- Earning a certain amount of money.

Concentrating on a certain goal sometimes means other things have to be given up.

Prioritising

Ironically, you'll finally understand the editor's point of view when the time comes that you yourself have to turn down work, particularly when there's no choice in the matter. Editors have no alternative but to return work when they've run out of space or there's lots on file, or that issue is on a particular theme. The writer unfailingly sees it as rejection. Initially, that is. You learn with experience never to take it personally, by which time you usually have so much other work to be getting on with, there's no time to brood.

Once you start to make a name for yourself, if your aim is to make a living from writing, you have little option but to turn down most requests for material when there is no payment. Obviously, there are exceptions to every rule, such as returning a favour or making a useful addition to your CV, but that's not much consolation. Writers seldom realise at first that it can be virtually as difficult, even embarrassing, telling somebody you cannot help them out, as it is to have your work returned.

Writing, pure and simple?

Just as some writers have one ambition, whether to win a poetry competition, have a novel published or see their article in a national newspaper, some have so many irons in the fire they're likely to get their fingers burnt. Problems with being a writer-of-all trades arise because it's easier to pigeon-hole people: Renaissance Man or Woman is not a term commonly used these days.

PRESS RELEASE

THE SHORT STORY WRITER'S SURVIVAL PACK
Everything you ever needed to know... probably.

Outlets, sources, events, organisations,
competitions, payment for publication
Tailored to suit individual requirements

Also available: ***The Poet's Survival Pack***

Carole Baldock (BA Hons) has been a freelance writer since 1993 and writes on a regular basis for a wide variety of magazines. She also contributes to the *Children's Britannica*, and American journals. Associate Editor of *Orbis*, an international quarterly of poetry and prose, Books Editor for both *Theatre Magazine*, and *Bigmouth*, her latest book is *Writing Reviews* (How To Books).

Send SAE for more details

Fig. 19. Sample press release.

We are all inclined to think that you need to possess a divine talent for any of the arts, although as actor Joe McGann says, it's just a job – the art is in getting work.

Staying flexible
We also assume that talent automatically reveals itself, and at a very early age. With so many choices in writing, you could begin concentrating on one form only to discover, years later, that all your experience and knowledge actually equips you for a totally different genre. It's quite easy to tell when you really are on the right track, since it tends to be the one where you have the greatest success, the one which could bring you fortune and fame – assuming that is what you want.

RESEARCHING THE MARKETS

As well as the various forms of writing, there are different fields to consider:

- literary
- popular
- technical
- educational
- humorous
- writing for children.

Nor are you restricted to only one area of expertise. For example: the background research for a novel can often be utilised for articles or interviews. A good indication of which is likely to be best for you is to consider the publications you read: which ones do you particularly enjoy, or find helpful, trade as well as newsstand publications? Once your work has appeared in a magazine, if you decide to try something new it may well be that the editor is more likely to let you go ahead. On the other hand, if you are known for a particular form of writing which goes down well with the readership, thoughts of the golden egg and the goose may come to mind.

IMPROVING RELATIONS

Editors can prove to be very good friends and they usually have your welfare at heart, since your success also reflects on them. They often go out of their way to help 'their' writers. Maybe you could offer your services, perhaps promoting the magazine or any of its related publications? Or, more simply, by keeping editors informed of any news that could be of use, even introducing like-minded editors to one another. In this way you can either help editors locally or act as a middleman when they live at opposite ends of the country.

The world of publications is vast and it's surprising how often you find yourself 'in the know', acquainted with facts of which others are totally unaware. You may assume that any editor will at least be conversant with editors of magazines in the same field, whether friend or foe, but this is not necessarily the case. Although there are often highly efficient networks operating between most editors, there are always a few who slip the net. If editors appreciate the help you give them, they are always ready to return the favour, helping you out in turn with useful information and contacts.

BECOMING A REGULAR CONTRIBUTOR

Writing a column

When is a column not a column? When it takes up half a page, or even a full page. Many newspapers have a number of columnists, specialising in different areas:

- politics
- entertainment
- sport
- women's interest
- topical events
- humour.

Some columnists are deliberately controversial, playing devil's advocate; sometimes you get the strong suspicion that the writer is having to follow the newspaper's official line rather than express what they really think. At one time the number one rule was *never* to concentrate on number one; columnists were meant to keep their personal life well and truly under wraps. This is no longer the case; some of what you might call 'personal columns' elicit the greatest response from readers.

Developing a column

Even if columns are not on a specific subject they often have a theme, although some are so vague there's a licence to tackle anything at all, such as 'Never trust anyone who...' in the *Sunday*

Times. Columns are also popular with writers. One small press magazine editor has always claimed it to be an ambition. Enjoyable as it is to be congratulated on a moving poem or a well-written article, since a column is so much more personal, compliments are all the sweeter. Most gratifying of all is when the editor leaves it entirely up to you to develop the column any way you want. Against that, when the publication schedule is particularly erratic, readers may think you yourself are unreliable. The biggest nightmare, however, is having to come up with something to discuss. But, like even the most difficult piece of writing, once started it usually works out fine.

Writing a series

Running out of ideas is a greater problem still with a series, as there is so much more space to fill. After all, anything promoted as 'a major new series' is likely to mean a two-page spread, so if you are ever tempted to suggest tackling this form of writing, before dropping hints to the editor make quite sure that you have enough material for at least twelve months ahead.

One solution is when you start having books published, as it's relatively straightforward to adapt chapters as articles. You'll also probably be allowed to include a mention of the book, thus promoting it. Indeed, it is fairly common in writing magazines for an author to contribute an article about their latest publication, perhaps offering some free copies. One trap to avoid here is quoting the title in every single paragraph; no matter how interesting the rest of the article, such blatant name-dropping annihilates credibility.

There are several advantages in writing a series:

- regular income
- readers get to know you
- material for a book.

Given patience, this has to be the easiest way of getting a book out, though there will be a need for updating anything from the start of the series.

EXPANDING YOUR HORIZONS

Knowledge is what you yourself have learned; information is what other people want to learn.

> **Even if your great love is writing, and nothing but writing, consider what skills you have acquired.**

Maybe you are in a position to pass your skills on to others who want to find out more about writing. It should at least provide you with a regular income, but balance this against the fact that you will have far less time for writing and possibly less motivation. Anyone involved in teaching worries about draining their creative energy. Some of those prone to suffer from writer's block admit they have taken the easy way out, since other work is a good excuse not to get on with your own writing.

Running workshops or courses

Learning creative writing is extremely popular, whether by belonging to a writers' circle or attending a workshop or course. Quite a large number of writers' groups are set up by the former members of a workshop or writing class, with the advantage, for many people, of a social side. This, however, isn't every writer's cup of tea but no matter what kind of writing is your main interest, it is certainly worth sampling one or more of the above. You're bound to learn something, even if it turns out to be that you really do prefer to teach yourself. Some people are cynical to the point of believing that now they know why it's said that 'those who can do, those who can't, teach'. Yet they're unlikely to come away without gaining something useful in the way of information, if not contacts.

Many teachers have impeccable credentials, though the more famous they are, the more people attend the class as fans rather than would-be writers. Others seem to have more of a knack of showing others how to do it rather than being renowned themselves in a particular genre. Fortunately, there is often a wide choice, with as many as two dozen writers' groups in one city alone, plus a variety of classes run by different organisations:

- continuing education
- night classes in local schools
- WEA (Workers' Educational Association).

SETTING UP AN APPRAISAL SERVICE

Not everybody relishes the thought of having to deal with an entire

COMMONWORD MANUSCRIPT READING SERVICE

About the Service

Commonword's Manuscript Reading Service is open to anyone who lives in North West England. It provides writers with constructive criticism about their work, which may take the form of poetry or fiction (this does not include purely factual autobiographies or memoirs). Writers are given advice on how to improve and develop their work and, where appropriate, how to get it published.

Each manuscript is read by two trained readers (experienced writers themselves), who produce written reports about the work to be returned to the writer. This whole process takes approximately three months.

The Cost

The scale of charges

(a) for a short collec
sample chapters:

    Waged = £30

(b) for a full length no
stories (up to 15):

THE CAPRICORN INTERNATIONAL AUTHORS' GUILD

PRICORN INTERNATIONAL AUTHORS'

International Authors' Guild is an organisation
sional advice and personal guidance, publication
d many other benefits.

om International Authors' Guild is for anyone
vriting, from the beginner to the established auth
particular interest to the new writer who may not
egin. Perhaps you are a parent who has written s
children and think that other children might like
nsure about how to get them published. Perhaps y
nd would like to see it in print. Maybe you have
fiction in magazines and would like to have a
you are a writer who has already been published,
g that the editor who once accepted your wo
sted.

at does it do?

e Capricorn International Authors' Guild is commit
luable and personal service to writers of all ages an
blished or unpublished.

Offering its members.....

FLAIR NETWORK

SERVICES TO WRITERS

Flair Network offers a complete service for
writers of all ages, abilities and aspirations.
Cas and Janis Jackson, both published
writers, poets and lecturers, have combined
their skills and expertise to offer professional
yet friendly advice on all aspects of writing.
Full details inside.

FLAIR NEWSLETTER
FREE ADVISORY SERVICE
FLAIR COMMENTS
FLAIR HANDBOOKS
FLAIR YELLOW PAGES
FLAIR AUDIO TAPES
FLAIR MANUSCRIPT SERVICE
FLAIR ASTROLOGICAL SERVICE
PUTTING THE PAST ON PAPER
HOW TO WRITE YOUR FIRST NOVEL

FLAIR FOR WORDS

Fig. 20. Appraisal services.

class of people, and may prefer working on a one-to-one basis. Providing critiques or appraisals is a service which is becoming more and more popular and there is clearly a demand for it. What exactly is a critique? 'A critical examination' (Chambers), a critic being 'one skilled in estimating the quality of literary work'. An appraisal: 'to estimate the worth of'.

In fact, both processes go a lot further than that, since their main purpose is to assist would-be writers with advice and information. For example, prose, characters, dialogue, plot and structure will all be examined, and details of events and outlets provided. It is important to also remember that even well-established writers may require such a service when they want to brush up certain skills or acquire new ones. All kinds of appraisal services are on offer:

- courses and workshops
- writing organisations
- writing magazines
- freelance writers
- competition organisers.

Using an appraisal service
Increasingly, writers who go in for competitions are offered the option of having an appraisal of their entry. This ranges from a tick sheet to one or two A4 pages of in-depth analysis and, obviously, the cost varies considerably. Appraisals can be expensive, so always double check to find the one best suited to your needs.

Providing critiques

Once you yourself are fairly well-established, it may be worth considering supplementing your income by running an appraisal service. There is a lot of competition, but there are even more writers who want somebody to help them with their work. You may have discovered that you have an 'eye' for the technicalities of writing, be it straightforward proofreading or the complexities of editing, which ranges from checking the basics like grammar and spelling, to suggesting how the contents could be polished until they shine. Indeed, in doing this kind of work, you yourself can gain a greater understanding of the various forms of writing and learn a great deal about applying different methods to improve your own work. There are, however, a few disadvantages;

- extremely time-consuming
- not always very well paid

- apt to interfere with your own work
- requires a lot of motivation and diplomacy.

Giving encouragement

If you are taken on by a writing organisation, the main priority is *not* to discourage the person who has submitted their writing. Naturally, you should also keep this in mind if you should opt for a one man band operation, by providing 'constructive criticism'. Unfortunately, a number of would-be writers are so convinced they are destined for fortune and fame, their ambition blinds them to the necessity of learning to walk before they run. Some people also find it difficult to differentiate between writing for themselves and writing work for other people to read, *ie* the ability to communicate.

However, finding the best way to suggest improvement can be very satisfying, whilst discovering a genuine talent is nearly as exciting as your own successes. Nonetheless, charging people huge sums of money in order to inform them in purple prose and words of several syllables that they are the very best thing since sliced bread (regardless of the actual quality of their work) is the kind of con-trick operated by the vanity press.

CASE STUDIES

Dexter worries about losing face

One morning Dexter calls into his local bookstore, to do some market research. The manager, who has always been very helpful, introduces him to a German writer, on holiday in the UK. He has been enquiring about the possibility of their stocking his latest poetry collection and whether they know anyone who writes reviews. Dexter is overwhelmed by the other man's enthusiasm and rather envious of all the awards he says he's received. He asks Dexter to undertake a six-month project, promoting the book – for a handsome payment, plus all expenses. When the review copy arrives, he is horrified to find that the contents are pretty dire. Shelley-Danielle has to remind him that this is an opportunity to put his command of the English language to the test, and 'sell' the book.

Brent thinks there's a job opportunity staring him in the face

Brent is asked to do a feature on the local college, whose brochure has a remarkable number of different subjects. What really surprises him are the interviews with some of the teachers. He discovers that the main priority is their ability to teach, rather than loads of qualifications: the man who does Writing for Radio has only had a couple of jingles on the airwaves; the one teaching Stand-up Comedy appears to have no sense of humour whatsoever. As for the lady doing Publishing Your Short Stories, she admits this is hypothetical because although she has written several, she's never got round to submitting them, being so busy with this course. Brent wonders if the college would be interested in running Aspects of Today's Novel.

Katrina's face doesn't seem to fit

Katrina's item about a certain publication appears in one of the best known writing magazines and, as the editor is extremely pleased, she naturally submits a couple of suggestions. Unfortunately, these are turned down as not quite suitable, and the next couple of ideas cannot be used since there is enough on file for the next eighteen months. Subsequently, Katrina keeps reading about the same magazine 'welcoming freelances', until she finally rings one editor to explain that these details should be updated because she's been told there aren't any opportunities. The editor points out that the information has come directly from the other editor.

DISCUSSION POINTS

1. What successes have given you the most satisfaction in the past year?

2. Which aspects of your work do you find most frustrating?

3. Given the choice of one particular field, how would you like your writing to develop?

ASSIGNMENT

Draw up a five-year plan (or three years, or whatever you feel is realistic), showing what you should like to achieve in that time. Now list what's coming up in the next twelve months and compare the two, to see what adjustments may be required.

9
Moving Up

Producing a book is a giant step for most writers. This chapter spells out what's likely to be involved:

- the different areas: non-fiction; poetry; prose
- approaching a publisher
- preparing your manuscript
- proposal acceptance, and payment in the post.

PUBLISHING NON-FICTION

No matter what poetry awards you win or which prestigious magazines publish your work, nothing gains you as much respect as having a book published. Everyone always assumes your new book is a work of fiction, but non-fiction, too, puts that something special right at the top of your CV.

> **In fact, non-fiction publications are the logical starting place, because this is where writers are most likely to succeed.**

Admittedly, non-fiction may not be where most writers plan their first success, especially poets or novelists, but if you've ever found yourself weighing your favourite author's latest blockbuster, wondering how many words per pound, remember that non-fiction books can be as few as 10,000 words. Rather less daunting than anything approaching six figures, unless that happens to be profit.

Handbooks or information packs range from 4,000 to 10,000 words and are very popular, covering a wide range of subjects. In the educational sector they are aimed at GCSE and A-level, and publishers are usually interested in suggestions for new ideas.

Being a contributor

If you fancy something smaller, investigate the possibility of contributing to a work of non-fiction:

- reference books
- dictionaries
- encyclopaedias.

This may involve submitting short essays, often biographical, but payment varies considerably as does the amount of research. Some publishers provide all the necessary background information, others expect you to live in the library.

Submitting non-fiction manuscripts

The non-fiction market is huge so it should prove quite easy to choose an area (or several) which interests you so much you could write a book about it. Make sure that you have the right publisher for the right topic, and that they aren't about to publish a book on the same subject. A preliminary phone call should be sufficient to see if they are interested in your proposal. If so, forward the following:

- covering letter
- CV
- market research
- outline
- sample chapter (sometimes two).

The outline sets out, step by step, what each chapter covers: *ie* the list of contents. The covering letter should be as short and sweet as you can make it but could incorporate enough personal details to render a CV unnecessary. This tends to be the case whether you have, as yet, gained few credentials, or whether they include some choice morsels. Once work is published in well established magazines, or is written for prestigious companies, your CV enters the realms of quality rather than quantity. As a books editor, there's little point in listing every magazine for whom you wrote reviews, apart from those of which you are particularly proud.

Using your market research

Some publishers ask you to complete a publicity form at the same time as signing the contract. It will contain all your relevant background details, to help provide information about possible

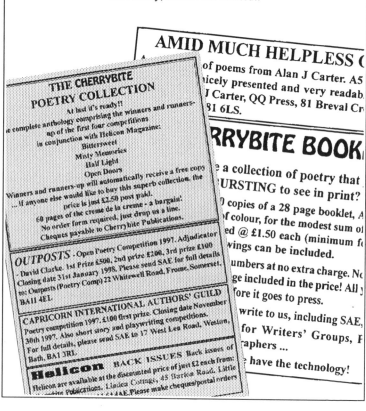

Fig. 21. Sample ads from publishers, genuine (*Cherrybite*) and vanity.

contacts in the media. This is where scrupulous market research comes in, for by now you will have some idea of whom you should approach to promote your book, as well as keeping an eye on the opposition.

PRODUCING POETRY COLLECTIONS

Many writers set off with some idea of having a book published 'one day', while some never even imagine such a thing. According to one magazine editor, it is the writing and the poetry that matter, not the getting paid or being published, though maybe it's just as well the contributors don't think along the same lines. It does seem to be true that the best poems are created because they *have* to be written. It's an entirely different matter trying to summon something up solely to submit for publication and/or payment. Naturally, commissioned work is an exception, but this involves experienced poets who have the know-how to conjure up excellent writing.

As soon as many people see their poems in print, their main aim is to have a collection published, maybe a booklet to hand out to friends and family. The over-ambitious see themselves in the running for fame and fortune, and Poet Laureate to boot. It is far easier to have a book of poems published than it is to get work accepted for the better small press magazines, and since a book is clearly a huge step up from a magazine, an awful lot of people manage to delude themselves about the quality of their work.

Selling poetry collections
Any unknown poet who thinks 500 copies of a collection will be snapped up learns the hard way the real meaning of the phrase 'flogging a dead horse'. Even poets who are reasonably well known, from the regular appearance of their work in magazines and themselves on the performance poetry circuit, find that selling poetry books is like trying to give away stale turkey sandwiches the day after Boxing Day. In a word, marketing and selling a poetry book is a million times harder than getting it published. You are up against enormous competition and promising 'short cuts' seem tempting.

You can never please all the people all of the time because poetry means very different things to different people. It's a jungle out there: if it isn't the fans of verse dead set against the fans of free verse, then it's page versus stage (poetry published or poetry performed) and it has *always* been the 'accessible' against the 'wilfully obscure'.

PUBLISHING FICTION

Succeeding with short stories

Having short story collections published has more in common with poetry than with novels, as stated in Chapter 6. Success is not completely unattainable but usually comes with being an established name. The writer renowned for short stories is held in high regard, as esteemed as the best poets, yet blurbs in publishers' catalogues seem strangely indulgent. Either a debut collection is regarded as but a step towards the novel or it's a question of a novelist being allowed to experiment.

As with poetry, the simple answer is to become thoroughly acquainted with the small press world, aiming to have your work anthologised. The main publishing houses occasionally bring out collections of 'The best of...'. You stand a better chance if you happen to be of Scots or Irish descent – rarely Welsh, for some strange reason, and never English. Irvine Welsh has done a great deal for the short story, though much of his work is what Ramsey Campbell calls 'anecdotal', even reworking very old jokes.

Looking at market forces for novels

> 'Write about what you know' is the usual advice, but for a publisher to give your work serious consideration write about something the public wants to know.

With the unexpected runaway success of Jung Chang's *Wild Swans*, the result was 'wild horse syndrome'. Nothing could drag the major publishing houses away from the idea that the public wanted more of the same, *Bound Feet and Western Dress* (Pang-Mei Natasha Chang) and *One Thousand Chestnut Trees* (Mira Stout) being just two of them. After the success of Patricia Cornwell, it was said that anyone submitting anything about a British female pathologist would be trampled in the rush of agents waving contracts. Following John Grisham, it was a lawyer.

To be ahead of the game, you need to be able to work out the next trend, but be warned when it comes to emulating a favourite writer. All writers are influenced, to some extent, by other authors, but Booker Prize winner Graham Swift came in for criticism because *Last Orders* was deemed remarkably similar to William Faulkner's *As I Lay Dying*, even if nobody did notice until after the ceremony.

Even curiouser: the bestselling writer who borrowed huge chunks from another, explaining that 'essentially random and non-pervasive acts of copying (were) attributable to a psychological problem'. As yet unnamed, this syndrome is probably known to most of us as 'cheating'.

Considering the literary and the commercial

It's disheartening to find how many blockbusters are badly written, and poorly edited. One author, whose early books were highly praised but little known, is currently enjoying huge success because of a complete change of style. The books are now almost excruciating to read, clearly aimed at Hollywood where they are being turned into movies. There is always going to be a huge chasm between high and low brow, literary and popular, although many readers enjoy both. Everyone has different tastes and will plump for one or the other, whether Isabel Allende or Catherine Cookson. Some award-winning writers bridge the gap, like Roddy Doyle.

Novels by writers who predominantly write for themselves are likely to remain in manuscript form, no matter how much the author yearns for publication. Market research is essential, compromise inevitable. A book, after all, should be written with the intention of being read. People choose the books they want to read, which are not necessarily the ones you want to write.

> **The basis of economics is supply and demand; produce something which is what people are after, and it sells like hot cakes.**

APPROACHING A PUBLISHER

Catch 22: publishers don't look at anything which is not submitted via an agent, but agents won't take you on unless you've been published. However, there's no reason why you shouldn't ignore this truism and go right ahead: submit your work to either a publisher or an agent. Regardless of your track record, if it's good and, more importantly, providing it's the kind of thing they're looking for, it will be published. The new novelist is expected to have a much harder time of it than a seasoned author, but it is never wise to taking anything for granted in the writing business. There are cases of popular writers, with many books to their name, being dropped like a stone once they're no longer flavour of the month.

Using appraisal services

This is a third option which, for some reason, rarely appears in books or articles. Writing courses or workshops may lead to useful contacts, since they are often run by people who are in contact with publishers, as authors themselves, or working in a publishing house. An even better proposition is an appraisal service, as advertised in most writing magazines. To fully do justice to your work, it is always advisable to have a critique done. Unlikely to be cheap, it's worth it if you find that what you've produced, once polished to perfection, is suitable for publication, and 'you may like me to have a few words with somebody who could be interested?'

Again, do not take it for granted that this is bound to happen. It's for the fortunate few, where an expert is 100 per cent certain that they have a winner on their hands and can then bask in the glow of reflected glory.

PREPARING YOUR WORK FOR SUBMISSION

Some people advise that you may as well submit your entire manuscript, to give the publisher's reader a chance to appreciate the masterpiece as a whole. Yet anyone who reads unsolicited fiction will tell you that it rarely takes longer than the first paragraph, let alone the first page, to know whether to bother reading on. In general, make enquiries first, to find out what the policy is for specific publishers. They may indeed invite you to submit your manuscript, but more likely prefer to have a general idea of what's in store first. As with non-fiction, submit the following:

- covering letter
- CV
- market research
- synopsis
- three sample chapters.

These are usually the first three chapters, though some argue for an extract from the middle. The publisher gains the gist from the synopsis and shouldn't get confused; meanwhile, you establish that you can keep up the momentum.

Writing the synopsis

The synopsis is an art form in itself, to be studied thoroughly before any attempt is made to encapsulate your novel, describing it as fully as possible in as few well-chosen words as possible. In journals all articles are preceded by an **abstract**: a summary of the contents, enabling researchers to see at a glance whether the article will be of use. Unfortunately, writers are notorious for being incapable of providing abstracts of their own work. One basic mistake is to imagine that, like the book, you must keep the reader in suspense. The purpose of a synopsis is quite the opposite – you must reveal all, but in such a way that the publisher is able to judge whether or not it is worth reading.

DELIVERING YOUR MANUSCRIPT

When posting your submission to a publisher or an agent, make absolutely certain it's the kind of subject area in which they specialise. Double check also that you have strictly adhered to the rules of presentation, which include enclosing a big enough self-addressed envelope with the correct amount of postage stamps attached. Once it arrives, the first person to retrieve your masterpiece from the slush pile will probably be a junior or a freelance, whose mission is suspected to be tossing as much as possible lightly aside. Fortunately, human nature being what it is, even the most cynical reader secretly hopes to unearth a hidden treasure. Due to the rarity value, they'll get some of the glory for discovering a new bestselling author.

Anything promising goes to a more senior editor, who then pleads its case at a meeting, to justify publication. At this point, your potential as a marketing tool is assessed since people need persuading to buy new novels so a 'hook' or good angle is required: an author who has led an intriguing life or pursues unusual hobbies.

COUNTING THE COST

Nowhere other than publishing will you be expected to produce something, and then wait up to a year for any kind of remuneration. Small publishers rarely have sufficient cash flow to operate any other system, but sometimes make twice-yearly payments rather than paying annual royalties. Alternatively they send the first royalty cheque a matter of months after publication, the second to be paid on a set date each year.

Making advances
On acceptance, if there is an **advance** payment it is usually made in several instalments:

- on signing the contract
- on delivering the manuscript
- shortly after publication.

You may also receive a cheque after a year, if initial publication was as a hardback and the book is then issued as a paperback. Royalties, usually ten per cent, will not be paid until the amount received from sales of the book exceed the advance; they may be increased to fifteen per cent if an agreed number of sales is reached. Best of all, you do not have to refund the advance, even if sales are below target. A publisher who does a print run of 5,000 copies, for example, with a total advance of £1,000 (£500, plus two payments of £250), expects every copy to be sold within a two-year period.

Self-publishing

Graham R. Stevenson, in *How to Write for Publication*, insists that subsidy publishing is a polite name for vanity press. However, if you build up a good relationship with them and share the costs, to end up with £2 for every copy of a book sold at £5 means you make a reasonable profit. With a popular book, in the long run you'll probably earn as much as you would with a 'proper' publisher. Self-publishing is now making quite a name for itself. Established authors such as Timothy Mo and Susan Hill have done rather well with it, though for a new author it's the usual uphill struggle. People are generally not interested in buying something they know nothing about by somebody they've never heard of. Marketing here is vital, because a self-published book which does sell in quantity means that the author has fewer overheads and makes more profit.

CASE STUDIES

Dexter discovers the meaning of poetic justice

Dexter brings out the classic slim volume of verse, working in collaboration with a local printer. Shelley-Danielle convinces him that the press release should describe him as a 'prize-winning local poet', although he has been so busy putting together his collection he has had little time for entering competitions, let alone winning them. In fact, the last one was run by his old school, for pupils past and present, but at least he came runner-up. She arranges for him to be interviewed by the local TV channel, who send along a junior reporter – the young man who won first prize.

Brent dines out on his achievements

Brent has always had an impressive CV, including the information that his work 'has attracted the attention of Channel 5'. He finally finds somebody who is fairly impressed with the synopsis of his novel and sample chapters, and will consider acting as his agent. They arrange to 'do lunch' so Brent can bring along the rest of his manuscript and tell the man all about himself. Including the fact that part of his CV actually translates as 'receiving the standard rejection letter from Channel 5'?

Katrina feels like booking in for treatment

Katrina has been books editor of a newsstand magazine for six months now and the 'child in the chocolate shop' feeling has not yet worn off. She's had to order loads of review copies because some of the bigger publishers are not very reliable, and she's been inundated with offerings from smaller presses. Then the editor suddenly closes her section down because she feels the readers are not that interested in book reviews. Although disappointed, Katrina can still study the publishers' catalogues to work out what kind of books are most likely to succeed.

DISCUSSION POINTS

1. What form of writing do you enjoy most or find easiest to do? Is there anything you do not like writing? How essential is it to your work?

2. If you have the patience to wrestle with a poem until it feels right, would you have the stamina to organise a collection? Could you go on to tackle a book of prose?

3. Do you dismiss other people's views when they read your work because they aren't writers? What about advice from professionals?

ASSIGNMENT

Collect catalogues from some of the main publishers. List the publications in each field: poetry, fiction and non-fiction. Categorise each type, *eg* for novels, crime, romance, *etc.* finally, make two lists: one of the most popular subjects and one of subjects you particularly enjoy. Is there the potential for a book, either fiction or non-fiction?

10
Publicising Your Book

This final chapter stresses the importance of marketing books and how to go about it:

- how to organise a marketing campaign
- working with your publisher, and producing press releases and review copies
- networking to get as much coverage as possible from your contacts.

ORGANISING YOUR MARKETING CAMPAIGN

Examine your CV. Every one of the people involved in publishing your work could be a marketing outlet, a source of potential customers for your writing. There are possibilities for promoting your book in all the following, so list those with the best chance for sales:

- publications
- broadcasting
- festivals and literary events
- writers' groups
- educational establishments (students and adult learners; writing courses).

> **It is essential for writers to help market their own book because of their personal interest.**

Publishers can have anything from dozens to hundreds of titles to take into consideration. It is not feasible for every book to receive the same amount of individual attention, but if *you* become actively involved the publisher will certainly appreciate your assistance.

COLLABORATING WITH YOUR PUBLISHER

While you make notes about marketing, along with those for your book, the publisher usually starts as soon as the proposal has been accepted. One thing to discuss on acceptance of the proposal is the inclusion of a **foreword**.

Including a foreword
Opinion seems to be split on the usefulness of a foreword. According to some writers it does little to promote the author or the book, yet many new books have a foreword. It's probably most useful for the first book, when it will help to establish your name. As the cover is designed early on, should you decide a foreword is a good idea, make arrangements as soon as possible. Try to obtain a couple of quotes as well; glowing recommendations come in handy for the press release and subsequent publicity.

Advantages
1.   A well-loved, well-known name on the cover attracts attention.

2.   An expert in the field adds authority and class to the book.

3.   It puts you in the publisher's good books, establishing your credentials as an author.

Disadvantages
1.   It can be very time consuming to arrange.

2.   You have to keep both 'name' and publisher happy with the result, never mind yourself.

3.   It may turn out to be rather different from what you had expected; it's one thing anticipating a few kind words – but you cannot dictate what those words should be.

Requesting a few kind words
At some point you are bound to have met people possessing the right amount of gravitas, if not fame, those whose name you casually drop into conversation, or ask to be a referee on your CV. Ask them for some kind of endorsement. When made with authority this should help sales, especially if the person doing the recommending is reasonably well known as an expert in the field.

Usually there is enough goodwill for a fellow author, even a celebrity, to be prepared to say a few kind words about your masterpiece, particularly if you happened to give their latest book a good review. As for unkind quotes, they have been known to be modified, with the bad bits cut out.

Quoting from experience: useful reviews

The media depend on politicians for sound-bites whenever another issue hits the fan; new books rely heavily on quotes. They reassure readers that they have made a good choice, because Mr SoandSo says so. Close study makes interesting reading since many writers are praised as the 'best writer of their generation', by another writer. Christopher Hampson received the ultimate accolade: *Les Liaisons Dangereuses* was unanimously decreed as 'brilliant': by *The Daily Telegraph*; *Financial Times*; *Guardian* and the *Sunday Times*. That's a brilliant piece of marketing.

Useful as it is for a budding crime writer to be hailed as 'the new Ruth Rendell', how much better if the doyenne herself adds her fivepenn'orth? Increasingly, quotes occupy a page or two inside new books, whilst covering much of the back cover, with a particularly impressive citation on the front. Publishers usually deal with these arrangements because of their contacts, possibly reciprocal agreements. You can let them know if you have someone particular in mind, and a good reason for making the request.

PROMOTING WORK THROUGH PRESS RELEASES

Make a list of suitable outlets for review copies: editors whom you know personally, and those who know of you, are usually willing to look at your masterpiece. Review copies are accompanied by a **press release** and if you want to be involved in writing it, inform your publisher in plenty of time. It may be possible to have an 'official' press release and one more 'reader-friendly' for your own contacts. All information must be accurate, with your achievements well presented. CVs are drawn up to create a favourable first impression, although some people are prone to poetic licence or get carried away with minutiae; even if you have had 137 poems published, in three different countries, it won't make people take you, or your writing, seriously.

Designing and making use of press releases

In some cases you can try the personal approach, enclosing a press release with a letter. If it feels like blowing your own trumpet, it would probably work better coming from the publisher. The use of a third party has a more convincing ring, being seen as unbiased as well as authoritative.

The press release is handled by the marketing department, but they usually welcome useful suggestions. Ask for a supply, to go to suitable destinations amongst your own correspondence, but keep them informed. It looks very unprofessional if you both send them to the same outlet, giving the impression that nobody has a clue what's going on.

Press releases can be scaled down to provide flyers, or up to make posters. There are usually plenty of suitable places for both but you need permission first before putting posters up. If you want to make sure they go on display, offer to do it yourself in:

- local library
- bookshops
- schools, colleges, university
- community centre; health centre
- galleries, theatres, museums.

USING REVIEW COPIES FOR PROMOTION

Making an offer they can't refuse

Nearly every publication these days includes readers' offers: speculate in order to accumulate. Few editors turn down anything which suggests 'value for money' to their readers, so don't miss out on the chance of publicity if it's possible to do an interview or a feature to accompany the offer. Similarly, depending on how well you know the editor, you can always suggest it yourself. Where the editor is already acquainted with the publisher, they may well come to some arrangement.

A small proportion of the print run is set aside for review copies, and a few more for 'freebies' should not go amiss. This is something you *must* discuss with your publisher first, before you inform all and sundry that of course they can have as many copies as they want. Most publishers will oblige; the press release sometimes mentions that copies are available as competition prizes or readers' offers. One problem: it's difficult to judge exactly how many books will be snapped up. The public may ignore a promotion, unless it's in a favourite publication; new magazines often have an extremely low response rate.

Following up enquiries

Making an offer which can't be refused is a good way of creating awareness, as well as monitoring interest in your book, so it's worth following up enquiries where possible. Courtesy costs nothing and the personal touch could persuade people to buy a copy if they were interested enough to try and win one. Feedback is invaluable to discover what is actually required but it's difficult to get a straight answer. People dislike completing even the simplest questionnaire and tend to write what they think you want to know. If you decide feedback is important, offer some kind of incentive in order to coax a response, a prize which is as enticing as you can afford, organised as some kind of raffle.

Running a competition

Competitions are another means of promotion, if the publisher is in agreement – when left to you to organise, remember it's a lot of hard work. The popularity of the lottery is a fairly good indication that most of us would like something for nothing. Hence competition questions nowadays tend to be as simple as ABC: what's the fourth letter of the alphabet and so on. What's much harder is promoting a competition, dealing with all the entries, and then having to judge them, or persuade or pay somebody else, since a famous name does wonders to encourage entrants. If this is an area where you have little experience it can go badly wrong, from nobody bothering to enter, to suggestions of fraud.

Requesting trade terms

Some editors may suggest offering your book at a specially reduced rate to their readers. The publisher can send them details of trade terms, *ie* making a discount depending on the number of copies the publication purchases. This kind of arrangement ensures a review since the publication, obviously, will want to sell copies of your book. The national press have their own 'bookshops' offering copies of the titles reviewed, often at a slightly lower price, for their readers' convenience. You may have noticed it's invariably the blockbusters from the big publishing houses; the smaller publishers also have good authors but they can't afford to join in this game.

CONTACTING OTHER PUBLICATIONS AND ORGANISATIONS

Your mailing list can be expanded to include the contacts which you have made in the course of research, and those listed in the various

WWN

The Newsletter of the
WOMEN WRITERS NETWORK

October 1997   Volume 13 Issue 2
Price £1.00 FREE to WWN members

A SEASON IN PARADISE

by Cathy Shaw

*Alice Walker wrote: "The most foreign country is within."
Dea Birkett, who quoted Walker in her book* Spinsters
Abroad: Victorial Lady Explorers, *may have recalled the line
many times during her months on Pitcairn Island...*

Dea Birkett's first book was her doctoral thesis on Mary Kingsley, a determined woman explorer of the last century. From *Spinsters Abroad* to *Serpent in Paradise*, about her four-month sojourn among the descendants of Fletcher Christian, Dea herself has had many adventures. Each of them, as she told WWN London at the September meeting, has been a journey of self-discovery.

The nature of travel writing has changed, and Dea Birkett has been in the vanguard of the movement. Travel writing Nick Hornby' of the travel world," which is quite a mishmash of genres and genders to hope for!

OUTSIDERS IN

Dea's books are thus as much about characters as places. She mused about having an unconscious pull towards writing about small, intense and misunderstood communities, like the world of the sailors she wrote about in Jella: A Woman at Sea, the story of working her passage back to England on a cargo ... ...frica. ... book ... on ... rcus.

Don't Miss a Meeting!

13 October – Serially Speaking. Gaynor Davies, Fiction Editor of *Woman's Weekly*, on the revival of interest in popular serials.

10 November – Making Book. Patrick Walsh, of the Crhistopher Little Literary Agency, on taking some of the gamble out of publishing.

No December meeting.

8 January 1998 – Speaker TBA.

12 February 1998 – Speaker TBA.

More details on the back cover

Fig. 22. Useful organisations and their publications.
(Women Writers Network, The Society of Women Writers
and Journalists and The Writers' Club)

sections of non-fiction books: Further Reading and Useful
Addresses. The latter is often sub-divided into Organisations and
Societies, Professional Associations and Services; by this point in
your career you may well have been invited to join one or more.

Getting into the editor's good books

It's important to keep up-to-date with market information, but not
all writers can afford to subscribe to every writing magazine. In the
small press it is common practice to swap adverts (and flyers), so
everybody benefits from information reaching the widest possible
audience. Any publication included in your book will most likely
return the compliment, though there is no guarantee of a gushing
review, even if theirs is included as recommended reading.
Fortunately, bad publicity really is better that no publicity at all,
since it makes people aware of the existence of the book. At least
you should get a mention, even if it is invariably hot off the press
release.

News items are a useful entrée to all kinds of publications; a
single sentence can promote something, if it contains all the relevant
information. Study the ads in writing magazines and consider their
potential, particularly if it is for a publication or an organisation of
interest to you. Would-be contributors usually contact magazines
with a view to finding out what the latter can do for them, ie publish
their article, story or poem. This way you're a step ahead, because
you are offering the editor free promotion when suggesting you
write about their magazine. Even a short piece has greater appeal
than an advertisement because it's more descriptive, and anything
deemed impartial often gets a better response. Once you've made
both parties happy, providing interesting copy for one whilst
promoting the other, that's two more potential outlets.

Getting the timing right

With marketing you must always heed the calendar. Try to ensure
that your book is publicised at a time which has the maximum
potential. For example:

- educational books are published at the start of the academic year
- books on tourism and leisure appear as soon as people start
  planning their holidays.

Don't forget about your other work: most things accepted for
publication can include a mention of your latest creation. Non-

fiction writers soon notice how tightly the media are tied to the calendar: a collection of love stories, for example, will look completely out of place unless it appears around Valentine's Day or, at a pinch, Christmas.

Anything like this requires stringent forward planning, especially as every publication has its own particular lead time, (see page 93), so you should always check first with individual outlets. Allow at least an extra month on top of lead times when sending out press releases, to give the editor time to allocate a writer.

Using local radio

Of course, you are an ardent supporter of your local station... Not the one you have playing music in the background all the time, but BBC Local Radio. Start listening, or ring up and ask for their schedule so that you can pick out the programmes which may be useful, then contact the producer concerned. If your book has wider appeal, make a note of other radio stations which have a particular interest, for example those based in the same city as your Regional Arts Board or counties which have a high proportion of writers' groups or where the annual festival is a high profile event. With the latter there will be lots of local coverage, but an expert view from outside the area makes a welcome change. If it is somewhere you already have contacts, that in itself should prove a useful introduction. Possibilities for inclusion in a radio programme:

1. Being interviewed on an arts programme, discussing your life as a writer and, of course, your latest book.

2. Joining a debate with a local celebrity or a noted expert from another locality.

3. Commenting on local events: opening of new venue, anniversary celebration, festival.

4. Taking part in a phone-in, where you can use your knowledge and experience by answering listeners' questions.

Even if air time is only a few minutes, it's ample time to give your book a mention. If you don't manage to get on, make sure that press releases go to all relevant personnel. You can also suggest that the presenter uses the review copy as a listeners' offer, or provide a couple more copies, and the number of calls can be monitored which gives you some idea of the response. If there's a lot of interest it's worth targeting that area by approaching an assortment of publications:

- listings magazines
- local papers
- Sunday papers
- county magazines.

Apparently, the average number of calls is twenty to thirty, which may not seem a lot – until you multiply it by the number of radio stations throughout the country.

ORGANISING LAUNCHES

Champagne reception, slap-up meal in a posh hotel, hob-nobbing with celebrities, head-hunted by fans and publishers all the way from the US of A... Sorry, not yet. Once again, think local:

- library
- bookshop
- giftshop
- any club or society of which you are or were a member
- children's school
- your old school
- alma mater (university).

Think well ahead. Timing is vital, so organise the launch once books are available. Few things are more frustrating than being besieged with orders when you don't actually know when the book will arrive; things done on impulse aren't always followed up. Similarly, choose your venue carefully, somewhere there is easy access – always double-check the date and the day. If your book is sure to be a hit with students, don't launch it during the holidays.

Launches needn't be expensive, though a free lunch helps guarantee a high attendance (the wine always runs out, no matter how carefully you plan). If you have been able to get funding this sometimes includes a sum for 'hospitality', but if you're thinking of splashing out you'll need some kind of sponsorship, and that's a whole new ball game (another book entirely). It's probably best to regard the launch as a small celebration party, and friends and colleagues may rally round, contributing food and drink.

Celebrating your achievement

After all, you have plenty to celebrate: a book of your own, something with your name on, there on the shelf of your local library and the bookstore in the city centre. If you have been actively involved in marketing itself, all the more credit to you; just as every acceptance for publication is always a source of great pleasure to a writer, so is each successful promotion. The rewards of writing are many, whether it comes from seeing your name in print or from people recognising your name, to keeping your bank account in the black.

CASE STUDIES

Dexter takes charge

Dexter, much to Shelley-Danielle's annoyance, starts submitting news items to a writing magazine. At least it's something which brings in a regular monthly payment. The idea springs from a review copy sent to him by a small press magazine; their latest publication is an excellent book which he realises he could promote in a short piece, with information about their updated guidelines. It's the first of many and, eventually, another editor contacts him to ask if he will take over the section of his poetry magazine which deals with news, reviews and competitions. When the next issue is published, Dexter sees himself in print – as contributing editor.

Brent charges in

Brent realised when he started working on The Novel that he had ample material for a non-fiction book about the music industry. Somehow he never got around to doing anything about it – until he discovers that a book on the same subject has been published. And it's by a local writer, somebody Brent cannot stand because of their reputation for pinching other people's ideas; worse still, their writing is dreadful, nowhere near as good as his. Inspired (infuriated?) he lists suitable publishers and the first one he rings confirms that they don't have anything similar in the pipeline. Can he drop them a line? The initial process takes over twelve months but the book is finally accepted for publication.

Katrina charges towards publication

Katrina's cousin asks for help with her A-level coursework on the topic of teenage pregnancy. There is a lot of information, but it's extremely difficult to track down (not to mention embarrassing, as her cousin says, and she's not even pregnant). Shortly afterwards, Katrina's outline for a schools' information pack on desktop publishing is returned to her because it's already been covered. However, the publishers include a list of possible subjects, aimed at sixth form students. Katrina suddenly realises that there is a gap in the market: teenage pregnancy. She has plenty of material, enough, it turns out, for two packs on the subject.

DISCUSSION POINTS

1. How far do you think a writer should be involved in promoting their own work?

2. Would you like to have some say in drawing up a press release? What kind of things would you want to include?

3. Are there areas where you think your contacts may be more useful in promotion rather than leaving it entirely to the publisher?

ASSIGNMENT

Having divided your CV into various categories, even if it's as basic as poetry, prose, non-fiction, break it down further still by considering the various angles covered in your writing (education, health, leisure, arts and so on). Make a list of magazines which specialise in one of these areas.

Glossary

Abstract. A condensed version of a piece of writing.

Advance. Sum of money made by some publishers on acceptance of a book proposal, to be set against future royalties; paid 'in advance' of the book being written.

Appraisal (critique). Assessment to improve work, making it publishable standard.

Blurb. Sometimes over-the-top promotional piece of writing, on the back of books, in flyers and press releases.

Copy. The prepared typescript submitted for publication, prior to being typeset.

Copyright. Written work 'of sufficient length' is automatically copyright. Ideas (and titles, because they are too short) are not, and should therefore be put in writing rather than discussed over the phone. Lasts seventy years from the end of the year of the author's death.

Cover sheet. Attached to the front of submissions, advising title, word count, name and address and offering FBSR (see below). Not always essential but can act as an invoice.

Critique. See Appraisal.

CV (curriculum vitae). A summary of your life. Writers should restrict themselves to relevant details.

Deadline. Editors' and writers' worst nightmare: the final date for submitting work.

Filler. Item of limited length, used to 'fill' gaps in magazine layout.

First British Serial Rights. Offering the right for work to be published for the first time, and once only, in Britain.

Foreword. Introduction to a book, recommending same, written by an authority or celebrity.

Genre. Specific category of writing such as horror or romance.

Guidelines. A list of publication requirements, to which would-be contributors must adhere.

House style. Rule book used by publication/publisher to ensure consistency in text.

Human interest. That irresistible, gossipy element which fascinates readers and keeps them taking the tabloids and magazines.

Independent press. More commonly known as small press, though this term is becoming more popular. Hundreds of literary magazines are available on subscription.

In-house. Copy written by the office staff of a publication.

Kill fees. A sort of consolation prize when work commissioned is not actually published. Amount is at the discretion of the editor, ranging from 100 per cent to token fee. The work may then be sold for publication elsewhere.

Lead time. The latest date it is feasible to submit suggestions to a publication.

Libel. A malicious or defamatory statement which has been printed or broadcast.

Listings, listings magazine. A form of directory, which in a listings magazine includes details of entertainments during the coming week.

Mailing list. Database maintained by organisations, containing names and addresses for receipt of information.

Mainstream. Traditional or current subjects.

Market research. In-depth study of possible publication outlets, vital for all writers.

Marketing. Creating awareness; using publicity to promote a newly published book.

Networking. Building up contacts; an informal collection of people committed to helping one another and thus helping themselves.

Newsletter. A leaflet or booklet produced by an organisation, from companies to clubs; promotes and provides information.

On file. Curious state of limbo regarding work submitted to magazines which is retained for possible future publication, *ie* not suitable for immediate acceptance but not rejected outright.

Outline. Proposal for a piece of work, stating its purpose, with brief details of contents.

Press pack. Provides background information about new films, performance and so on. Often includes photographs.

Press release. Promotional material issued to the media and other interested parties.

Public Lending Right. Minute amount payable to registered authors each time their books are borrowed from libraries.

Readership. Those who regularly subscribe to or purchase a particular publication.

Slush pile. 'Affectionate' term for the heap of unsolicited manuscripts with which publishers have to contend. Despite dismal track record, *ie* next to no works of genius uncovered, writers, primarily novelists, continue to live, and submit work, in hope.

Small press. See Independent Press.

Source. Origin of information.

Topical. Anything dealing with the burning issue(s) of the day, whatever hits the headlines.

Vanity press. Companies which prey on the vanity of inexperienced writers, assuring them of fame and fortune in order to make a fortune themselves.

Further Reading

b = bi-monthly; m = monthly; q = quarterly; t = twice-yearly; tt = three times a year; w = weekly.

REFERENCE BOOKS

Research for Writers, Ann Hoffman (A & C Black, 1994).
Willings Press Guide (IPC Business Press, annual).
Writers' & Artists' Yearbook (A & C Black, annual).
The Writers' Companion, Barry Turner (Macmillan).
The Writers' Handbook, ed. Barry Turner (Macmillan/Pen, annual).

BOOKS ON WRITING

Bestseller: Secrets of successful writing, Celia Brayfield (Fourth Estate, 1996). Inspirational, whilst emphasising what hard work writing a novel really is.

Copywriting for Creative Advertising, by J Jonathan Gabay (Hodder & Stoughton Teach Yourself series, 1996). Extremely useful when it comes to ideas for marketing.

Freelance Writing, Chris Moore (Robert Hale, 1997). One of the most useful guides for those who take writing seriously.

From an Editor's Desk, Suzanne Ruthven (Ignotus Press, 1995).

Getting to Grips with Writing, Catherine Hilton and Margaret Hyder (Letts Educational, 1995). Other titles: *Punctuation and Grammar; Spelling; Vocabulary.*

How to Publish Yourself, Peter Finch (Allison & Busby, 1997).

How to Write a Blockbuster, Sarah Harrison (Allison & Busby, 1997).

How to Write Five-Minute Features, Alison Chisholm (Allison & Busby, 1995). Plenty of ideas in this step-by-step guide; a little classic.

How to Write for Publication: An introduction to successful freelance writing, Graham R Stevenson (Arrow Business Books, 1997). Covering all the nuts and bolts to provide an excellent start to building up your career.

How to Write and Sell a Synopsis, Stella Whitelaw (Allison & Busby, 1993).

How to Write Stories for Magazines, Donna Baker (Allison & Busby, 1996).

The Magazine Writers' Handbook 1997/98, Gordon Wells (Allison & Busby, 1997). Indispensable for those specialising in non-fiction, especially in conjunction with his other title *The Craft of Writing Articles* (Allison & Busby, 1996).

The Poetry Business, Peter Finch (Seren, 1994).

Starting to Write, Marina and Deborah Oliver (How To Books, 1996).

Unpublishable!, Elaine Borish (Fidelio Press).

Writing a Novel and Getting Published, Nigel Watts (Hodder & Stoughton Teach Yourself series, 1996). A thorough and encouraging exploration of the whole process.

Writing for Magazines, Jill Dick (A & C Black, 1996).

Writing for Pleasure and Profit, Michael Legat (Robert Hale, 1995). Note that 'profit' takes up all of one chapter. Nonetheless, very highly regarded.

Writing for Publication, Chriss McCallum (How To Books, 1997). First-class market-by-market approach; not surprisingly, it is now in its fourth edition.

Writing for Reader's Digest (Reader's Digest, Berkeley Square House, Berkeley Square, London W1X 6AB). Provides some good advice.

Writing for the BBC (Broadcasting House, Portland Place, London W1A 1AA).

Writing Poetry and Getting Published, Matthew Sweeney and John Hartley Williams (Hodder & Stoughton Teach Yourself series, 1997). Enjoyable, no-nonsense guide.

Writing Reviews, Carole Baldock (How To Books, 1996).

BOOK MAGAZINES

Bookseller, editor Louis Baum. (w), 12 Dyott Street, London WC1A 1DF. Tel: (0171) 836 8911. Fax: (0171) 836 6381.

Books in the Media, (w), Peter Harland, Director & Publisher, Bookwatch Ltd, 15 Up East Street, Lewin's Yard, Chesham,

Buckinghamshire HP5 1HQ. Tel: (01494) 792269. Fax: (01494) 784850.

Books Magazine (b), editor Liz Thomson. Free from bookshops. 43 Museum Street, London WC1 1LY. Tel: (0171) 404 0304.

WRITING MAGAZINES

Freelance Market News, see Useful Addresses: The Association of Freelance Writers.

The New Writer (b), editor Suzanne Ruthven. £29.50 pa (ten issues). PO Box 60, Cranbrook, Kent TN17 2ZR.

Writers Bulletin (b), editor Chriss McCallum. £20 pa (ten issues). PO Box 96, Altrincham, Cheshire WA14 2LN.

Writers' Forum (q), managing editor Morgan Kenney, £14.50 pa. 21 Belle Vue Street, Filey, Yorkshire YO14 9HU.

Writer's Monthly (m), editor Vivienne McKiver, £33 pa, PO Box 14, Taunton TA4 3YZ.

Writers News (m) plus *Writing Magazine* (b), editor Richard Bell. £41.60 pa. Writers News Limited, PO Box 4, Nairn IV12 4HU.

SMALL/INDEPENDENT PRESS PUBLICATIONS

Booklets/packs: useful sources of marketing information

Fiver Guides, series of writers' directories. *I: Poetry and Short Story Magazines that Pay*, Carole Baldock. £5. Cherrybite Publications, Linden Cottage, 45 Burton Road, Little Nelson, South Wirral L64 4AE.

Light's List, annual booklet. £1.50. John Light, Photon Press, 29 Longfield Road, Tring, Hertfordshire HP23 4DG.

Magazines: useful sources of marketing information

Always send an SAE

Lateral Moves, ed. Alan White. £2.00 per issue. Aural Images, 5 Hamilton Street, Astley Bridge, Bolton BL1 6RJ.

New Hope International (b), ed. Gerald England. £18 pa. Magazine, chapbooks and annual booklet, *The Review* (single copy £3.75), which covers lots of small press magazines and books. 20 Werneth Avenue, Gee Cross, Hyde, Cheshire SK14 5NL.

Orbis (q). ed. Mike Shields. Subs £15, single issue £4, back issues £2. Makes payment for poems. Poetry Index section includes magazine reviews and news. 27 Valley View, Primrose, Jarrow,

Tyne & Wear NE32 4QT.

Zene: The guide to the independent press (q), ed. Andy Cox. £8 pa, sample issue £1.95. 5 Martins Lane, Witcham, Ely, Cambridgeshire CB6 2LB.

Small/independent press publications which pay

Acumen (tt), ed. Patricia Oxley. £10 pa, single issue £4. Poetry, short stories, essays, translations, interviews, reviews. 6 The Mount, Higher Furzeham, Brixham, South Devon TQ5 8QY.

Books Ireland, literary editor Kevin Kiely. £20 pa for nine issues. Poetry, short stories, articles, reviews, artwork and photography. 800-1,400 words. 11 Newgrove Avenue, Dublin 4, Republic of Ireland.

Chapman (q), ed. Joy Hendry. £14 pa, single copy £3.50. Poetry, reviews and critical essays. 4 Broughton Place, Edinburgh EH1 3RX.

Defying Gravity (b), ed. Craig Turner. £10 pa, single copy £2. Poetry, prose, arts reviews. Gravity Publications, 26 Tomsfield, Hatfield, Hertfordshire.

The Edge (q), ed. Graham Evans. £7 pa, £2.75 single issue. Short stories, reviews, articles and interviews. 111 Guinness Buildings, Fulham Palace Road, London W6 8BQ.

Helicon Poetry Magazine (q), ed. Shelagh Nugent. Poetry. £2.50 per issue (£9 pa) Also publishes *Peninsular Magazine*: short stories. Cherrybite Publications, Linden Cottage, 45 Burton Road, Little Neston, South Wirral L64 4AE.

Lochs (q), ed. Rafael Kimberley-Bowen. Five issues £6.90, sample copy £1.50. Humorous short stories, poetry, spoof news items, cartoons, articles, interviews. Kimbo International, PO Box 12412, London SW18 5ZL.

New Welsh Review (q). ed. Robin Reeves. £15 pa (two years: £28), single issue £3.60 + 60p p+p. Poetry, short stories, features, reviews (cinema, theatre *etc*). Chapter Arts Centre, Market Road, Canton, Cardiff CF5 1QE: Tel/fax: (01222) 665529.

The North (t), ed. Peter Sansom and Janet Fisher. £10 pa; single copies £5.50. Critical articles, reviews, poetry and occasional fiction. The Studio, Byram Arcade, Westgate, Huddersfield HD1 1ND. Tel: (01484) 434840. Fax: (01484) 426566.

Poetry London Newsletter (tt) extensive listings. £9 pa, 26 Clacton Road, London E17 8AR.

Poetry Monthly, ed. Martin Holroyd. £12 pa, single issue £1.50. Articles which are commissioned receive payment (negotiable), poetry and reviews. 39 Cavendish Road, Long Eaton, Nottingham

NG10 4HY.

Poetry Now (q), ed. Andrew Head. £14 pa, single issue £3.50. Poetry, news, reviews, interviews, articles. 1-2 Wainman Road, Woodston, Peterborough PE2 7BU.

Poetry Wales (q), ed. Robert Minhinnick. £12 pa (two years: £22), back issues £3 + 50p p + p. Poetry, features, reviews. 11 Park Avenue, Porthcawl CF36 3EP.

QWF (Quality Women's Fiction) (b), ed. Jo Good. £20 pa, £3.75 single issue, back issues £2. Short stories and articles; critique service offered. 80 Main Street, Linton, Nr Swadlincote, Derbyshire DE12 6QA.

The Rialto (b), ed. Michael Mackmin. £10 pa, £8 low income; £3.90 single issue: current issue free on payment, as subs run from the next one published. PO Box 309, Aylsham, Norwich NR11 6LN.

Stand (q), ed. Lorna Tracy. £11.95. Poetry, short stories, reviews. 179 Wingrove Road, Newcastle upon Tyne NE4 9DA.

Staple (tt), eds. Don Measham and Bob Windsor. £10 pa (£5 concs), £3.50 single copy (back issues £3 for two). Short stories and poems. Submissions three months before publication (March, June and December). Contributions to: Bob Windsor, Gilderoy East, Upperwood Road, Matlock Bath, Derbyshire DE4 3PD. Subscriptions: Donald Measham, Tor Cottage, 81 Cavendish Road, Matlock, Derbyshire DE4 3HD.

Story Cellar (tt) £10.50 pa inc free entry to three annual competitions. The editors, 26 Cippenhall Lane, Slough, Berkshire SL1 5BS.

the third alternative (q), ed. Andy Cox. £10 pa, single copy £2.75. Or subscribe to *Zene* as well for a total of £16. Short stories, articles, artwork. TTAPress, 5 Martins Lane, Witcham, Ely, Cambridgeshire CB6 2LB.

Magazines that don't pay but look good on your CV

Envoi (tt), ed. Roger Elkin. £12 pa, back copy £4, sample copy £3. Poems, articles and reviews. 44 Rudyard Road, Biddulph Moor, Stoke on Trent ST8 7JN.

iota (b), ed. David Holliday. £8 pa, single copy £2. Poetry, reviews, lists books and magazines received. 67 Hady Crescent, Chesterfield, Derbyshire S41 0EB.

Smoke, ed. Dave Ward. £2 for three issues; 50p single issue. Poetry and artwork. Windows Project, 40 Canning Street, Liverpool L8 7NP.

Tears in the Fence (e), ed. David Caddy. £9 pa for three issues, single copy £3.50. Poetry, stories, reviews, articles and essays. 38 Hod View, Stourpaine, Blandford Forum, Dorset DT11 8TN.

Xenos (m), ed. Stephen Copestake. £16.50 pa. Short stories, good feed-back section. 29 Prebend Street, Bedford MK40 1QN.

Useful Addresses

ORGANISATIONS AND SOCIETIES

ALP (The Association of Little Presses), c/o 111 Banbury Road, Oxford OX2 6JX. Web site at hhtp://www.melloworld.com/alp £12.50 pa, includes: *Palpi (Poetry and Little Press Information)*, twice-yearly booklet, usually £5, a quarterly newsletter and the current catalogue of the biennial *Little Press Books in Print* (normal price £3.75, inc p + p).

A-PN (Author-Publisher Network), press officer John Beasley, South Riding, 6 Everthorpe Road, London SE15 4DA. £12 pa. Publications include *Small Publishers A-Z: The guide to good publishing*, Daphne Macara.

The Friends of the Arvon Foundation, Joan Thornton, 6 Church Street, Darfield, Yorkshire S73 9LG. Tel: (Arvon Foundation) (01422) 843714. £5 pa. Regular newsletter, markets, literature, competitions, events and courses.

The National Small Press Centre, BM BOZO, London WC1N 3XX. £12 to join, subs include six issues pa of *News from the Centre*, four of *Small Press Listings*; otherwise £6 pa and £10 pa respectively. Offers various services: resources, book ordering, advice slips and so on.

The Poetry Society, 22 Betterton Street, London WC2H 9BU. Tel: (0171) 250 4810. Fax: (0171) 240 4818. London £20 pa, elsewhere £15. Wide range of benefits for members including *Poetry Review Quarterly* and information bulletin.

Public Lending Right, Bayheath House, Prince Regent Street, Stockton-on-Tees, Cleveland TS18 1DF. Tel: (01642) 604699. Fax: (01642) 615641. Note closing date for applications: 30 June.

PROFESSIONAL ASSOCIATIONS

The Arts Council of Great Britain, 14 Great Peter Street, London

SW1P 3NQ. Tel: (0171) 333 0100. Produces a quarterly bulletin, *Writers Available for Tour*, which contains other useful information. Contact Sarah Sanders in the Literature Department, x6234.

The Society of Authors, 84 Drayton Gardens, London SW10 9SB. Tel: (0171) 373 6642. £70 pa. Wide range of services, including a free quarterly magazine of 100 pages; *The Author* is edited by Derek Parker, available to non-members at £6 per issue.

The Society of Women Writers and Journalists, Joyce Elsden, Hon. Membership Secretary, Nash Manor, Horsham Road, Steyning, West Sussex BN4 3AA. London £25 pa, regional £21; £10 joining fee: variety of services.

Women Writers Network, Cathy Smith, Membership Secretary, 23 Prospect Road, London NW2 2JU. £30 pa: services as for SWWJ, entry above.

Workers Educational Association (WEA), National Office, Temple House, 9 Upper Berkeley Street, London W1H 8BY.

The Writers' Guild of Great Britain, contact for details of rates: 430 Edgware Road, London W2 1EH. Tel: (0171) 723 8074. Official magazine *The Writers' Newsletters* (10 issues pa), ed. Patrick Campbell.

SERVICES

The Association of Freelance Writers, The Writers Bureau Ltd, Sevendale House, 7 Dale Street, Manchester M1 1JB. Tel: (0161) 237 1827. £29 pa. (11 issues pa). Services include appraisals, competitions, 11 issues of 12-page newsletter *Freelance Market News*, editor Angela Cox.

Book Trust, The Publicity Officer, Book Trust, Book House, 45 East Hill, London SW18 2QZ. Tel: (0181) 870 9055/8. Fax: (0181) 874 4790. e-mail HUWbkinfo.demon.co.UK. Send (6½ x 9) sae for newsletter and full details.

The Capricorn International Authors' Guild, D G Tutton, West Lea Road, Weston, Bath BA1 3RL. £35 pa. Services include professional criticism and guidance, competitions and market information.

Commonword and Cultureword, Cheetwood House, 21 Newton Street, Manchester M1 1FZ. Tel: (0161) 236 2773. Advice on all aspects of writing and publishing for groups and individuals.

Directory of Writers' Circles, Jill Dick, Oldacre, Horderns Park Road, Chapel-en-le-Frith, High Peak SK23 9SY. Tel: (01298)

812305. e-mail jillie@cix.compulink.co.uk. £5, post free; 8th edition.

Flair for Words, Cass and Janie Jackson, 5 Delavall Walk, Eastbourne BN23 6ER. £10 pa. Services include appraisal and advisory service, newsletter (six issues), audio tapes.

The Greeting Card Association, 41 Links Drive, Elstree, Hertfordshire WD6 3PP.

Midland Exposure, Lesley Gleeson and Cari Crook, 4 Victoria Court, Oadby, Leicester LE2 4AF. Tel: (0116) 271 8332. Fax: (0116) 281 2188. Agency for commercial short stories, charges 15 per cent commission, also offers advice and encouragement. Send sae for guidelines, or phone.

Oriel (Welsh Arts Council's Bookshop), Peter Finch, Oriel Bookshop, The Friary, Cardiff CF1 4AA. Offers services to writers and small/independent press.

Pantomimes in June, 6 Mosslea Road, Bromley, Kent BR2 9PS. Tel/fax: (0181) 460 2280. £25 for 80-page non-fiction package for freelances, including regularly updated list of features editors. Send sae for details.

Poetry Library, Royal Festival Hall, South Bank Centre, London SE1 8XX. Tel: (0171) 921 0943. Fax: (0171) 921 0939. Free membership. Information service including lists of magazines, competitions, groups *etc*, available on receipt of large sae.

Real Writers, PO Box 170, Chesterfield, Derbyshire S40 1FE. Registration fee: £10; fee for monthly assignment: £15. Correspondence course. Send sae for details.

The Writers' Club Limited, Park Terrace Courtyard, Park Terrace East, Horsham, West Sussex RH13 5DJ. Tel: (01403) 210074. Fax: (01403) 249948. Subs £36 pa. Monthly newsletter plus bi-monthly magazine *Foreword*, members' directory and a directory of writers' services. Writing courses and exclusive offers such as discounts for workshops and free entry to twenty-three competitions a year (publication plus cash prices of up to £1,500). Also makes payment for articles and short stories (not poetry).

Index